DEAR CHARITY,
I'M DELIGHTED
YOU ORDERED MY
BOOK BECAUSE I CONSIDER
YOU A LADY WITH SUCH A
HIGH LEVEL INSIGHT TO FORGET THAT
I ATE GREATLY NOT TO FIND IN HIM - THAT EVEN
ALSO, WE'RE SISTERS FOR YOU TO FIND EVER
MY HOPE + PRAYER IS TO GUIDE YOUR EYES
WITHIN THESE PAGES, YOU'RE ALREADY
MORE INSIGHT. I KNOW WOMEN WITH DESIGN SMARTS!
AHEAD.

X.O.!
M.tw
3•6•2019

Design Smarts

Copyright

Design SMARTS
Inspiration for Home+Life

Mitzi Beach

All rights reserved. No part of this publication may be reproduced, distributed, or transmitted in any form or by any means, including photocopying, recording, or other electronic or mechanical methods, without the prior written permission of the publisher, except in the case of brief quotations embodied in reviews and certain other non-commercial uses permitted by copyright law.

Scripture taken from The Message. Copyright © 1993, 1994, 1995, 1996, 2000, 2001, 2002. Used by permission of NavPress Publishing Group.

ISBN: 978-1-949856-10-1 (paperback), 978-1-949856-11-8 (epub)

Brookstone Publishing Group
P.O. Box 211, Evington, VA 24550
BrookstoneCreativeGroup.com

Ordering Information:
Special discounts are available on quantity purchases by corporations, associations, and others. For details, contact Brookstone Publishing Group at the address above.

Design Smarts

Inspiration *for* Home+Life

MITZI BEACH

DISCLAIMER

This book and the information contained herein are for informative purposes only. The information in this book is distributed on an "As Is" basis, without warranty. The author makes no legal claims, express or implied, and the material is not meant to substitute for legal, medical, or financial counsel.

Nothing contained in this book is intended to be, or should be considered as, medical advice or a substitute for medical advice, diagnosis, or treatment. You should not disregard any advice provided to you by your medical or mental health providers, or delay seeking treatment from them, based on any information contained in this book.

The author, publisher, and/or copyright holder assume no responsibility for the loss or damage caused, or allegedly caused, directly or indirectly, by the use of information contained in this book. The author and publisher specifically dis-claim any liability incurred from the use or application of the contents of this book.

All rights reserved. No part of this book may be reproduced or transmitted in any form or by any means, electronic, mechanical, photocopying, recording, or otherwise, without the prior written permission of the publisher.

Throughout this book trademarked names are referenced. Rather than putting a trademark symbol by every occurrence of a trademarked name, we state that we are using the names in an editorial fashion only and to the benefit of the trademark owner with no intention of infringement of the trademark.

I dedicate this book to my husband, Bob,
who has never ever waivered in his
confident belief in me or in us.

Introduction

Did you know that you were designed to thrive, not merely survive? Can you actually get your ahead around that? A stronger, more fulfilled, more fun-filled and healthier life is possible for you no matter what are your circumstances? How do I know this can be true for you? Well personally, even after really tough times of financial woes, serious medical setbacks, discouraging career reversals, and relational disappointments, I not only survived but I thrived through it all. And you can too! You just need the SMARTS to make it happen. And this book is your essential resource to show you how.

Every person in every demographic can benefit from pondering this question: How can I thrive and not just survive in the midst of a changing America? There is a tsunami bearing down on us. The aging population is growing. Every single day, 10,000 people turn 65 and enter into the crumbling social security system. And not only that, but every day, according to social scientists, at least 12,500 Americans will turn 50 years old. That means, by the year 2030 over 40% of Americans will be past the half-century mark.

In this book, I will refer to this growing and immense segment of the U.S. population as the O50s.

We are living longer than ever, therefore, it has become increasingly relevant and essential for the wellness of this immense population group to discover fresh, new ways to thrive and enjoy their later years. O50s, are not yet in the geriatric segment, but are most definitely in this untapped and mostly neglected, in-between stage of life.

> "These people are the true social pioneers. Like 'Age Scouts', they travel ahead into the later years to chart the uncertain territory of long life."
>
> —Ken Dychtwalk, *Age Wave*

But Mitzi, you might say, you're an interior designer, why are you writing this book? My answer may be a surprise. Yes, I design spaces. I love color and shapes. But after thirty years of working with clients to make their personal and professional work spaces a place of beauty, comfort and function, I have come to see that all of life is about DESIGN. Throughout my entire career I have been privileged to design clients' homes, **but my lifelong passion has always been to do, and to be more for them.** So now I have taken my passion for design and transferred it to the six DESIGN SMARTS principles in this book which will hopefully inspire others to design their lives to do more and be more at any age or life stage.

In every single design project, there are sometimes countless numbers of intentional choices to be considered. It is understood that each and every choice will either enhance or compromise the end design project. In order to protect their financial investments, clients very rarely leave these choices to chance. It is not a reality for homeowners to naively assume or hope their project will magically turn out to be all they envisioned, without personal involvement.

It may seem an obvious metaphor to compare design projects to life, but please do not miss the most important point, which is that design

Introduction

projects reflect *intentional* choices. Nothing is designed without deliberation and consideration. Living a life of intention likewise requires you to live a life by your choices.

But how do you discern where to even begin the process of choosing what is valuable versus the daily life of busyness and your endless to do lists? My untiring hope is that you will choose to consider implementing the principles of DESIGN SMARTS to enlighten, equip, and empower your perspective on living as an O50. You will also find in this book that there are not only chapters, but it is also divided into topics as well. Because the stages of life are a series of transitions, I devised the acronym—S.M.A.R.T.S. as a guide to navigate these various and often treacherous transitions of life.

This book will take you on a journey of doable possibilities with an entirely unique and fresh perspective of living a life with DESIGN SMARTS. I believe without a shadow of doubt, there is always the choice to do better and to be better each and every day. This is, in no way, a prescription for simply living longer; It is to equip and to empower you to thrive, to be well and age well just as you were designed to do.

I am very excited to have you on this journey with me learning and reading of my own O50 story. You will also be learning of the beautiful stories of those who are indeed breaking those outdated and small-minded beliefs on aging in America today. This enlightened concept on aging embraced by the O50s is no fleeting idea. A bold, new approach to aging is emerging. I am beyond grateful that you are joining me!

> "In your home and by your lifestyle,
> you were meant to thrive, not merely survive!"
>
> —Mitzi Beach

S.M.A.R.T.S.

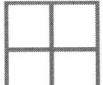 **SPACES.** Our spaces directly impact our lives. What is working in your home now? What is not?

 **MINDSETS.** Our lives directly follow our thinking. A positive mindset results in a positive life; a negative mindset results in a negative life. You get to choose.

 **ATTITUDES.** Our attitudes directly affect all and everything we do or become in our life. Age is just a number and you get to choose your attitude toward aging.

 **ROUTINES.** Our personal lifestyle in achieving wellness directly impacts our lives. Are you putting yourself first regarding your own personal life? You get to choose.

 **TOGETHERNESS.** Our relationships directly affect our quality of life. Giving back to your community and others changes everything. You get to choose to live outside of your inner circle connections.

 **SPIRITUAL.** Our personal decisions about spirituality affects our outlook on life. Everyone believes in something—either your own power or a divine power.

CONTENTS

BLUEPRINT: DESIGN PHASE

Chapter 1   Design Smarts: The Wholistic Approach to Downsizing...... 3
Chapter 2   They Did Not See Us Coming... 9

SPACE: CONSTRUCTION PHASE

Chapter 3   Is Your Home Your Friend or Foe?.. 21
Chapter 4   Downsize SMARTS- No One Wants Your Stuff 33
Chapter 5   The O50s Wish List 47
Chapter 6   Does Your Home Have A Soul?.. 61
Chapter 7   Healthy Home = Healthy Life 73
Chapter 8   The Housing Revolution Is Upon Us................................... 83

MINDSETS: LIGHTING PLAN

Chapter 9   An Awakening.. 99
Chapter 10 Above All, Get Wisdom.. 113

ATTITUDE: SELECTION PHASE

Chapter 11 A Cluttered Mind No More 133

ROUTINES: IMPLEMENTATION PHASE

Chapter 12 Wellness Redefined: Health is the New Wealth................. 151
Chapter 13 Simple Routines Versus Complicated Plans 163
Chapter 14 Easy Eating and Cooking Plans with Design SMARTS ... 173
Chapter 15 Can Your Furniture Sabotage Your Wellness?.................... 193

TOGETHERNESS: ACCESSORIZING PHASE

Chapter 16 A Path to Joyful Living 205

SPIRITUALITY: FINISHING PHASE

Chapter 17 Everyone Believes in Something 221

BLUEPRINT

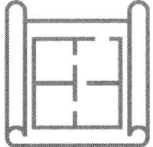

Design Phase

CHAPTER 1

Design Smarts: The Wholistic Approach to Downsizing

I am an interior designer writing a book about designing your life. In this book, I am going to tell you my story. I am also going to teach you to embrace downsizing with an entirely new perspective since this is the overarching theme of sizing your life for your now and for the life you will eventually live. To fully understand my purpose for writing this book, I hope that you will have read the introduction that explains the DESIGN SMARTS concept as I move forward with you in the chapters ahead.

I have designed homes both large and small, various types of medical offices, a TV station lobby, executive suites, and lake homes. I have worked with singles, married couples with children and those without children. I have worked with much older clients and much younger clients. I have worked with the fun, way-out there creative types, plus the very serious, left-brain individuals that just want me to give them the bottom line of costs involved. I have experienced successful financial years in my design business and years of financial drought. I have worked for other interior design businesses and have had my own interior design business for over 30 years.

A very essential part of my life as an interior designer, is to attend conferences throughout the country to enable me to speak with many people in addition to my own design clients. I am a firm believer that to keep current on trends, it is also essential to listen to what people are saying. Lately, I keep hearing one word repeated: DOWNSIZING.

My own personal take away is that an awareness of the various life stages is the beginning of wisdom.

We can make the 70's be the new 50's!

When I started to dig deeper into this concept, I did what I always do to further get a grip on other connotations of a word: I do research. Imagine my surprise when looking up downsizing revealed these synonyms:

- Economizing
- Trimming
- Downscaling
- Reducing
- Slim down
- Cut back
- Scale back
- Scale down
- Streamlining

There it was! After all of these years of interior designing and having lived through most of the life stages, I am astounded at how much of life relates to downsizing. The title of this chapter is: Design Smarts: The Wholistic Approach to Downsizing so it would be also logical to also looking up the meaning of wholistic:

Design Smarts: The Wholistic Approach to Downsizing

> "**Wholistic** refers to the whole, a whole item or whole body of a person or thing. The word defines the consideration of the entire structure or makeup, which includes the body, mind and the spirit in the case of a human being".
>
> Stackexchange—www.stackexcahnge.com

I will show you how a wholistic approach to downsizing relates and connects to each letter on the DESIGN SMARTS acronym in the following chapters. This was a light bulb moment for me, and I truly believe that it will be for you as well!

The first letter of the SMARTS acronym is S. S is for SPACE. Did you know that your home can extend your longevity? The keys to unlock these doors to longevity are detailed in the chapters on SPACE.

Did you know also that your lifestyle can extend your longevity? The keys to unlock these doors of longevity are detailed in the chapters on ROUTINE.

Did you also know that the other letters in the SMARTS acronym—Mindset, Attitude, Togetherness and Spirituality also affect your longevity? I believe the DESIGN SMARTS keys to unlock your happiness and fulfillment are surely possible. Why can I make these statements? It will become crystal clear, as I share my own personal life journey along with my years of study and research as proof that yes, these DESIGN SMARTS keys can work for you too.

Connect the Dots

Each chapter concept: SPACE, MINDSET, ATTITUDES, ROUTINE, TOGETHERNESS, and SPIRITUALITY represent only the tip of the iceberg on what is yet to be discovered on aging. Obvious, also, is the fact that I could only partially write about health, home, and attitudes as, of course, there are literally volumes of material on each one of these major topics.

But the main thing is the main thing, and which is how essential it is that we receive, understand, and put into practice these DESIGN SMARTS principles in our daily lives. The entire DESIGN SMARTS message to achieve the ultimate Power can be summed up in two words: **GET PREPARED!**

TENACITY + EFFORT+ DISCIPLINE +SACRIFICE
= GREAT REWARD

This is a formula for any life endeavor. Why not apply it to aging as well?

Why work hard on healthy lifestyles only to slip and fall in the bathroom? A slip and fall can lead to major and long-lasting chronic issues, such as a back or head injury. Or what good is it to say yes to embracing the research that expounds that our attitudes and mindsets do affect our aging, but still continue an unhealthy lifestyle? No, we must incorporate all three areas to live wisely in our best years.

DESIGN SMARTS concepts are based on three basic areas to achieve the rewarding, powerful life we all want and deserve.

our **ATTITUDES**   our **LIFESTYLES**   our **HOMES**

ALL of the DESIGN SMARTS principles are wrapped up in these big three concepts. My ultimate passion and goal for you is that you get prepared in your attitude, your lifestyle, and your home for what is the inevitable fact of life: AGING.

Think of a three-legged stool, with each leg representing either our attitudes, our lifestyles, or our homes. Take away one of the legs and what happens? No stability; it's wobbly and weak. All three legs provide stability, security, and strength.

Remember, all of life is a choice. Yes, ALL OF LIFE IS A CHOICE. What we think, how we talk and how we act in our daily lives.

So, pat yourself on the back if you are now considering how you will choose to spend your future best rest years. Even this one small step of thinking about your future will put you way above most who never give a thought to preparing for their futures. I predict that if you are now thinking and considering your daily choices, your life is going to change for the better.

The Cliff Notes version that I concluded in my study is that all of life's stages require preparation and knowledge. My own personal take away is that an awareness of the various life stages is the beginning of wisdom. We should be prepared for what is unfolding now in addition to what potential the future holds. If I had only known of these life stages earlier in life, I believe I could have prepared myself more effectively rather than living with unrealistic expectations of life's various stages. It was time to take DESIGN SMARTS and move into the 21st century.

> "You're blessed when you meet Lady Wisdom, when you make friends with Madame Insight. She's worth far more than money in the bank; her friendship is money in the bank."
>
> —Proverbs 3:13

CHAPTER 2

They Did Not See Us Coming

Let's begin with my story. I believe it will open the doors into a wholistic approach that will relate to downsizing.

At 18 years old, I moved away from my hometown of Salem, Ohio with a population of 12,000 to attend Ohio University with 18,000 students. I remember my orientation like it was yesterday. I was nonchalantly listening, but attentive nevertheless, to the dean of students when he said something that struck panic into my freshman heart. I truthfully panicked. I was already insecure being out of my cocoon where, like the old TV show says, "Everybody knows your name".

"Look to the person to your right and to your left," he said, "at least one of you will not be here to start the second semester."

Yikes! I am going to flunk out of my freshman year at Ohio University! This cannot possibly happen to me. My parents had worked hard to send me away to college. My grades in high school were all A's or B's except for a few classes like French. My teacher was not only French, but we all thought she was well past her prime. At the time, she was probably much younger than I am as I write this book.

Why would he say that to me? I am a nice person plus I was already super homesick having never been away from home other than for family vacations or to camp with close classmates. I never even had a babysitter because with our large family we did everything together and took care of each other. Finding the courage to leave home was tough enough. Now I hear that they are trying to get rid of me! How can this be happening, simply because there were too many of us? We were the baby boomers, an emerging demographic. And now thousands of us were old enough to hit college campuses all over America. Therefore, various educational institutions had to eliminate thousands of students off their class enrollments due to facility limitations. Of course, at the time, I had no notion that this was the reason why hundreds of us would not survive our freshman year, so I freaked out!

Looking back at this regrettable situation colleges were dealing with, I am perplexed as to why colleges were caught unaware of our sheer numbers. Why hadn't they prepared for the largest group in history to enter their campuses? I have no idea and I remain equally perplexed as to why America has not prepared better for our large, aging demographic either. Or for that matter, why have we not prepared for the vast number of Americans turning 50 in America every day?

The highly respected author, Ken Dychtwalk says in his well-known book, *Age Wave*, "We weren't prepared for the boomers; there weren't enough hospitals or pediatricians. There weren't enough bedrooms in our homes, schoolteachers, textbooks or playgrounds. The huge size of this generation has strained institutions every step of the way." He argues that boards of education had 13 years to see us coming but instead he and millions of others had to go to class in shifts. "What was the surprise there?" he asks. He also notes that by 2020, the population of Americans age 55 to 64 will have grown an unprecedented 73% since 2000. This is a very huge ramification for all of us!

In my work as an interior designer I have had the opportunity to speak to many, many people. I have observed two things that parallel Dychtwalk's statistics: America is not prepared for the aging of its population and sadly, those individuals over 50 are not prepared individually either.

Author and columnist Gail Sheehy refers to the mid-50's to the early 70s as the "Grand Tweens" saying that these "pioneers and pathfinders among us" will shape this new stage of life, characterized by a renewed sense of purpose. I certainly agree. Being the ultimate, optimistic O50, I say, "Well, we have changed so many aspects of American life, why not change the way we deal with getting older."

We can make the 70's be the new 50's! But it can only be accomplished through preparation and planning, not wishing. Arianna Huffington, president and Editor-in-Chief of AOL Huffington Media Group agreed. "F. Scott Fitzgerald's line that 'there are no second acts in American lives' is completely wrong," she said. "As we grow older, we have the opportunity to tap into the kind of wisdom that is denied to the young—the opportunity to look at life without all the extra anxiety and self-judgment that dominated our lives when we were younger."

What makes the O50s so uniquely different?

The O50s are set apart from previous generations that had settled, often with a despondent resignation, into accepting their pattern of aging was normal and could not be changed. The majority of these prior generations expected a lessening of life's choices or opportunities. This is a very sad state as I witness them embracing their predisposed attitude of: This is just the way it is to get old so just buck up and accept it. What an unfortunate and mostly depressing scenario. Never let this description on aging be your attitude or your words! Now you can be the part of the new MOVEMENT with DESIGN SMARTS to be the change that defies all those ugly discouraging beliefs on aging.

Will it be easy to fight those old patterns of aging? No! It will definitely not be easy to fight the glass ceiling of aging in America. As thousands of older workers have been let go, often merely due to their age, starting over will be the challenge. I have many friends that this very thing has happened to, and sadly, it is often impossible to prove age discrimination. Perhaps some of you reading this book will be emphatically shaking your O50 head in agreement. I realize this aging battle is the O50s' challenge given our country's lack of respect or lack of confidence in the value and wisdom gained by hard work and perseverance.

Personally, I have been rejected for potential opportunities due to my age. Being overlooked was acutely painful for me knowing how much I could contribute. Being older has its own set of challenges to face, but to be categorized as useless or out of touch hits our self-confidence hard.

Substantiating how little the O50s are regarded, it is shocking to most people to find that less than 20% of the billions of dollars spent yearly on marketing in America has been directed to those over 50 years of age.

Recently I attended the very prestigious Kitchen and Bath show in Las Vegas where again I witnessed down right incorrect marketing which was bypassing the wealthiest and most powerful demographic in America, the O50s. In a PowerPoint presentation of the launch of a high-end appliance line, I observed the slide proudly announcing their targeted focus was the GenX demographic, those 35 to 50ish. What? My adult kids are in that demographic and they are not going to be buying a $10,000 range! The majority in this demographic is looking at college costs, extra cars and insurance for their teenage kids, orthodontics, sports and activity expenses to name a few huge financial costs of raising kids.

The bigger insult came when I tried to tactfully discuss why their marketing was targeting the wrong demographic. Guess what demographic these two marketing team members were age wise? Yes, you guessed it. They were millennials who were barely listening to me as some out of touch older lady who knew absolutely nothing about marketing. I asked them if they knew anyone over 50 and one said, sure, my dad. Mind you, upon inquiring their age it revealed they were in their early twenties working out of the New York City marketing office. I would bet my paint chips that they were brand new hires with no demographic research whatsoever.

But take heart, you O50s. The MOVEMENT is indeed happening in America!

Fortunately, marketing to the lucrative O50 demographic is increasing due in part to recognizing the vast profit windfall for those companies who are now acknowledging the power, influence, and wealth of the O50s. This overdue and way too slow to accept paradigm shift is also due to the fact that we O50s are making ourselves known in all trades, politics and industries. Look at Cher, Diane Keaton, George and Laura Bush, Bill Clinton, Dolly Parton, Kevin Costner, Maria Shiver, Erin Brockovich, and Steve Wozniak. More importantly, we are valuing the fact that we are becoming a mighty force in America! It is so exciting to witness a new, emerging, culture taking America by storm and demanding more and more options be available like clothing, housing, and even shoes! Yes, the O50s now are emerging as a force to be reckoned with and we now call it the MOVEMENT.

> "Never doubt that a small group of thoughtful committed citizens can change the world. Indeed, it is the only thing that ever has."
>
> —Margaret Mead

But wait, what is the big deal? Is this over-due recognition of the O50s all that necessary? The obvious answer is a resounding YES! As the above quote affirms, a calculated commitment will make change happen. Nothing in life that is of any long-term value just happens or is given to us and aging differently is a perfect example. If you are going to taste this new, pioneer lifestyle, you must be willing to change at least in your MINDSETS and in your ATTITUDES. But you do not have to figure it all out on your own because DESIGN SMARTS' goal is to equip, empower, and enlighten all you O50's with tangible tools to prepare you for your future years.

Do You Live Your Life by Your CHOICES?

In answering this seemingly unassuming question, "Do you live by choice or chance?" your answer will clearly reveal where you are mentally in your current life cycle? Another way to ask this question is: are you a planner or do you live by the seat of your pants just hanging on for dear life? For me personally, especially in my earlier life stages, I often did not have a clue!

Throughout my life journey, I freely admit that my own life would have benefited from these DESIGN SMARTS principles. In fact, now it is crystal clear to me that all life stages require preparation with the empowering knowledge of what can be expected. I am not qualified to know if most individuals have the foresight to prepare for their next life stage. I am qualified to report that during most of my life, I definitely lived by the seat of my pants just trying to hang on while trying to maneuver each stage.

You know the phrase if only I knew then what I know now? Boy, would knowing then what I know now have helped me even as a newly married young woman living away from my family and friends. This is not even close to the story I told of my freshman year at college since that experience was not a life-long commitment. We had moved to New Jersey from Ohio for Bob to start his career as an engineer in the oil business with me as a new high school teacher. Sounds like the perfect scenario to start out married life, right? Wrong! I was desperately unprepared and unequipped to have the slightest idea how to be a new wife. I had no counseling or advice from anyone, anywhere. At that time marital counselling was not wide spread. If it were our life would have been a much smoother ride instead of living by the seat of my pants.

Fortunately, being a learning junkie, I kept taking classes, going to conferences, reading whatever pertained to life stages in our homes and in our health. Thankfully, I was the benefactor during those years of seeking for more and more life skill understanding. I decided to not just let life happen, but to be instrumental in how to steer my own life. I elected to choose my life path as much as I could control. By acknowledging the vast chasm of what I didn't know or understand in my life I still underestimated the mountain ahead of me and found it difficult to gain any traction and actually make a difference in others' lives. Fortunately, this has now changed as many people accept the fact that they now have an option to choose what their futures will be. My greatest joy would be to witness the DESIGN SMARTS principles become a tangible and effective guide for others to experience a deeper and richer life.

O50s are members of this uniquely historic demographic. Are you ready to make history? If so, then buckle up and be instrumental in influencing the world of all those around you! My ultimate purpose for writing this book is to give encouragement for you O50s to steadfastly acquire the necessary knowledge to increase your wisdom and understanding. This valuable understanding ultimately will result in your belief that anything is truly possible for those of you who believe and receive the empowering formula of DESIGN SMARTS

I cannot think of anything more exciting and cannot wait to hear of your successful achievements. This new lifestyle will bring you the sought-after rewards of living by your intentional choices, ditching that old way of living by chance.

"Everything is either an opportunity to grow or an obstacle to keep you from growing. You get to choose!"

—Wayne Dyer

REFLECTIONS

America is changing in every single area of life both in positive and negative ways.

1. What are the positive changes that excite you?

    Example: Technology or medical breakthroughs

    _____

    _____

    _____

2. In what areas of your life, due to your age, have you experienced feeling devalued or overlooked? _____

    _____

    _____

3. It is an exciting time, in many ways, to be aging in America. In what ways are you participating in this O50s life stage?

    Examples: travel or classes

    _____

    _____

    _____

S.M.A.R.T.S.

 SPACES. Our spaces directly impact our lives. What is working in your home now? What is not?

 **MINDSETS.** Our lives directly follow our thinking. A positive mindset results in a positive life; a negative mindset results in a negative life. You get to choose.

 **ATTITUDES.** Our attitudes directly affect all and everything we do or become in our life. Age is just a number and you get to choose your attitude toward aging.

 **ROUTINES.** Our personal lifestyle in achieving wellness directly impacts our lives. Are you putting yourself first regarding your own personal life? You get to choose.

 **TOGETHERNESS.** Our relationships directly affect our quality of life. Giving back to your community and others changes everything. You get to choose to live outside of your inner circle connections.

 **SPIRITUAL.** Our personal decisions about spirituality affects our outlook on life. Everyone believes in something—either your own power or a divine power.

SPACES

CONSTRUCTION PHASE

Chapter 3

Is Your Home Your Friend or Foe?

In the next 5 chapters, I will teach you how the DESIGN SMARTS principles on SPACE relate to the wholistic approach to downsizing.

If you "listen" louder, you will hear the millions of Americans intently discussing whether to move or remodel. It is like a collective roar happening in the homes of those over the age 50. Actually, this deafening noise is due to the constant conversations of those 78 million who are in this nagging state of indecision, questioning both the inevitable financial and lifestyle impact of moving or remodeling in order to downsize their lives. This thunderous sound is coming from the tectonic shift occurring in America with the MOVEMENT from the past status that comes with owning a larger home, to owning a smaller one. Without a doubt, this is changing absolutely everything in the housing industry, the real estate market, and municipalities. This huge wave of change in housing will be felt for a very long time as Americans in great numbers shift to new housing models.

Now is definitely the time to learn how to deal with this huge shift and implement DESIGN SMARTS principles to prepare for it. You do not want to wait too long and be caught unprepared or unable to make this life changing decision to move. This is exactly why keeping up with current trends can literally affect your bottom line.

However, I do have many friends and family that do not fit this trend of moving to a smaller home. They are totally satisfied with their current home and lifestyle. This is one of the reasons why I love the extremely popular HGTV show, *Love It or List It?* The premise of this show is that homeowners must make a decision to either stay and remodel an existing home or move to a new home. Sound familiar? This same, emotionally draining battle goes on in so many homes as we debate whether to keep our home and update or rip off the bandage and make a move.

This was not an easy decision for my left-brain, engineer husband who is not a big fan of change in the small things let alone something as big as a housing move! Knowing that left-brain individuals live their life based on logic, Bob needed to understand why our family home of 30 years no longer worked for us as empty nesters.

I went into the discussion armed with my DESIGN SMARTS principles and a tangible list of our current home issues that no longer functioned for our life stage needs. With these tools I was able to help Bob understand why listing our home was the best option. It was a lightbulb moment for him. For him and many others, the lightbulb does get turned on until the logical data of the DESIGN SMARTS principles changes their MINDSETS. This knowledge gave Bob the power to understand why it was our time to make this life altering choice and move.

We purchased a 3500 square foot home we lovingly named Cypress. And yes, we were often questioned how this new home could be an example of downsizing?

The answer is simple, and easily understood, once you grasp that the principles of DESIGN SMARTS are all about the precise functionality of our spaces and not merely the specific square footage.

Using DESIGN SMARTS principles, we strategically evaluated the defined purposes for every room. This is vastly different from assessing and unfortunately buying many outdated homes that still include those useless and outdated SPACES present in supposedly downsized homes. The S in SMARTS teaches you that the size of the home is only the tip of the downsizing iceberg!

> "More rooms, bigger spaces do not necessarily give us what is needed in a home. Houses should be designed to nurture not impress."
>
> —Sarah Susanka with Kira Obolensky, *The Not So Big House*

My home was definitely not my friend at this life stage!

When our three kids left our home for college, we took on a new identity. Just like so many Americans, we were now empty nesters. It soon became crystal clear I had entered a life transition stage that I was totally unprepared to handle emotionally. Not only was our nest empty, but my heart was empty, too. While experiencing the acute vulnerability of insecurity and loneliness, I completely exhausted myself attempting to act like I still had it all together.

Unfortunately, I was not equipped to comprehend my new life stage. I felt like a train wreck that was destroying my hopeful expectations to stay connected with my college kids, and my husband within this unwanted, but inevitable, life stage. I painfully knew that our lives had changed forever.

Thankfully we had all those memories of raising our twin sons and one daughter through fun, adventurous, bonding years that will forever be imprinted on my heart and mind. Those awesome, wonderful, heartfelt times of all the stages of raising a family, were cherished beyond what I could have ever imagined in joy and love that we were fortunate to experience.

But when the house emptied out, and the "launching stage" as I call it began, it all changed on a dime, and I was totally unprepared for how to handle it. I had absolutely no idea and was clueless what to do with all those feelings, especially when some of my friends were just elated at being empty nesters. They certainly could not relate to my utter hopelessness at my "now what?" question.

That "now what?" question was deeply haunting for me as an O50 desperate to survive this unwelcome reality of my new life status. How can I maintain my interior design image, which required a professional posture and a positive attitude, regardless of my personal life? Fortunately, remaining in this quicksand of an all-consuming self-pity, eventually and laboriously turned into righteous anger that got my fire back. My self-talk then was, "Don't tell me this is all there is to my life." No way was I going to stay here in this pit of despair, constantly experiencing this nagging angst and frustration about my current life status.

We've all heard the phrase "If it ain't broke, don't fix it." But if it is broken, well, by golly, get on with life and fix it!

Compounding other numerous life issues, I finally concluded that one of my main areas of discontent was with my home. As an interior designer, this was a monster of a problem since it no longer fit this unwelcome, albeit emerging, lifestyle. In addition, the constant reminder that this life stage, of raising a family, was over was like a low-level headache that wouldn't go away. My home and my life wore on me daily as I tried to cope by hiding or burying my emotions. As many can relate, this stuffing of emotions eventually took its toll in deeply negative, relational consequences. Layering onto the frustration with how our home was not working for this life stage, was the fact that our adult kids were not only moving out, they were moving on to locate across the country. This meant we most likely would be visiting them and not vice versa. What was the point of all these unused rooms that housed all those precious memories and stood constantly empty as a reminder like a painful splinter?

Oh, our original family house was beautiful, and I had done everything I could to make it comfortable and functional. But unlike my many clients' design projects, no walls could be moved to functionally change our home. I can hear some of my clients laughing because, to me, moving a wall is no big deal if the end results justify the effort and costs. The master bedroom and master bath were opened up a bit, but not enough to really make any big, life-changing difference. Trust me when I say there was no way.

When I am teaching or speaking on interior design, I routinely emphasize the concept that "Eighty percent of the time we live in only twenty percent of our spaces." Naturally, it just stands to reason that this twenty percent should be a fabulously comfortable and beautiful space that feeds our souls and meets our every need. This was certainly not the case in our own home. Again, to me the question that reverberated through my empty house was, "Now what?"

Providentially, during this period a friend planted the seed to buy a fixer upper and move into his neighborhood of older homes, with tons of trees and meandering streets that were admired by many of us in East Wichita. This got my fire back for sure! Change, adventure, and possibility now surged into hope. I was not going to stay stuck in the mire of staying stuck. Believing that my situation was not permanent, since an end could be in sight, miraculously, I was lifted out of that pit of despair and hopelessness. This can sound petty and selfish, but to me personally, it was so much more than our home not working. Living in our old house was a constant reminder that my life would never again be the same. It felt so overwhelmingly empty.

Buying and restoring our current home, we call Cypress, was the saving anchor which prevented me from falling into the hopeless abyss that so many O50s are mired in today. Perhaps the reason is that so many O50s accept and believe that their current situation is all there is. They don't believe there is a way to change things. Sadly, they resign themselves to accepting their unacceptable state of affairs. Obviously, the Cypress story is certainly out of the question for most, or at least the sane people! The point is to never give up. Change is possible.

The history of our life stage being included in this chapter on spaces is intentionally detailed in order to humanize the why we did what we did. To merely begin with all the tangible home upgrades and restorations involved would have missed the essence of this book, designing the life you want. Not only literally moving, as in only the physical aspect, but we were also moving ahead in taking action and not just accepting life's setbacks or new life stages with an attitude of this is just how it has to be. Throughout my entire life, I have routinely examined my current status with an analytical approach. For better or sometimes worse, I admit, I plotted my path to achieving the results I desired by making intentional life changes.

> "Great designs come in all shapes and sizes. I've seen lots of fabulous small spaces that are chic and stylish, and I've also seen some enormous homes that feel cold and have no style whatsoever. It's not just whether your home is big or small – it's all a matter of what you do with what you have."
>
> —Libby Langdon, Small Spaces Solutions

What we tolerate, we will never change

This adage was spot on with how I perceived our family home of thirty years. I knew that regardless of what had been remodeled over the years, I simply could not tolerate it anymore. My mindset kept returning to the question of why should the rest of our lives be spent in a home that no longer fits our needs or wants? What would be the harm of selling and moving? Millions of people do it all the time, so why shouldn't we take the leap of faith to move ourselves into a space that worked.

I know some of you are saying, "I've never heard of anyone being so spoiled that just because she did not like something, she felt she deserved to move." You are darn right! I did deserve it. Bob and I have worked hard, and no one handed us anything on a silver platter. And you also must know that after over forty-five years of marriage, we both continue to work hard to this very day. There is a time, I believe, in all our lives when the decision to "love it or list it," as the HGTV program emphasizes, is necessary. We've all heard the phrase "If it ain't broke, don't fix it." But if it is broken, well, by golly, get on with life and fix it! Even with the limited budgets that most of us have, I truly believe that there is always something that can be done to improve our situation. Examples would be de-cluttering, major cleaning, higher grade of light bulbs, painting, reevaluating how unused rooms can be repurposed for new functions, or even new accessories. These simple and certainly doable upgrades can be easily and inexpensively accomplished; which is why I say again, doing something is always possible.

But for Bob and me, we had already done all the changes we could possibly do to our old family home; therefore, moving was our game plan. I ask you, why stay in a home that no longer works for your life stage or is depressingly outdated? For many O50s, to remain in a home that is downright unsafe simply lacks wisdom. Even making modest improvements will help tremendously for the O50s who could be facing knee replacements, surgeries, or the myriad of other issues that make their present home nothing more than spaces where an accident is waiting to happen.

Changing seasons and changing life stages

One of life's realities is that friends come in and out of our lives, either at different life stages, or by moving to different locations. Of course, we all have lifelong friendships regardless of our ages or location; but generally speaking, this is the pattern of friendships. And often, it is the way it is meant to be. Let me explain. When our kids were young, I desperately needed my young mother friendships to help me maneuver all the challenges of motherhood living away from my extended family. Now that my kids are adults and parents themselves, those former friendships have faded. There are still the Christmas cards or occasional calls, but basically, they were critically needed and absolutely appreciated decades ago but now, different friendships meet my needs. And in turn, I truly attempt to meet their needs at whatever level is needed by my relationship with them. This analogy of friendships to our home being our friend or foe is clearly a relevant comparison to logically analyze, especially for the O50s moving into new life stage territory.

When you are living in a home, condo or apartment suited just for you, your gifts and your talents will be able to be released.

Do you remember the painful goodbyes of your friends moving away, or worse, dropping you like junior high friends did? Did it leave a sad void in your life? This chapter relates outdated friendships, or dissolved friendships, to living in homes that no longer serve your purposes or meet your needs. However, the enormous pitfall of living in homes that rob your joy or peace or worse, your quality of life is the temptation to do nothing about it. If you employ DESIGN SMARTS principles, you will not stay stuck in a home that no longer fits your life stage or your life style.

The question is again:
Is your home your friend or foe?

In the introduction to this book I cited the shocking and unprecedented American tsunami of O50s that is going to hit American shores. This huge wave will predictably change most facets in our country. For sure it will put an unprepared for, and challenging, strain (with major demands) on America's inadequate housing options. Therefore, the O50s, as they contemplate where they will live, will be asking themselves, "What are we going to do?" Surprisingly, the majority of this huge age group says they will age in place until they are forced to make a change. Here is the perplexing disconnect since most homes are simply not age friendly. Adding to this growing dilemma is the mindset of the O50s themselves. But as Nick Lehner, of the Architectural & Planning Firm, KTGY Group states, "We've been talking about this age wave for years, but no one's really doing anything about it. Builders are figuring it out as they go, for the majority; it's not something that becomes part of the conversation."

Why, then, are our needs not being met in our homes? Well, one of my often-stated theories is that we adjust ourselves to our spaces; instead of manipulating our spaces to fit our needs and ourselves. It is time to say enough! I want my home to work for me, not for me to have to adjust to make my home try to meet my needs and wants! It hardly ever works!

> "We shape our buildings; thereafter they shape us."
> —Winston Churchill

This disconnect between the O50's lack of realistically assessing their housing status, plus the building industry's overall lack of producing options, is the underlying passion and purpose for my never-ending commitment to the philosophy underlying all of DESIGN SMARTS. For over fifteen years, I have felt like a lone voice in the wilderness, but I steadfastly believed that change would indeed happen. Even though it seems like moving a cruise ship with an oar, my concern, my passion and my love for my fellow O50s, will never waiver.

> "Everybody lives someplace and they're all wanting to do something to change the way they live!"
> —Marie Kondo, *The Life-Changing Magic of Tidying Up*

What questions should the O50's ponder?

This is your opportunity to honestly assess your current home and answer these questions, not for anyone else, but for yourself and possibly your spouse/partner. But only you can discern your unique individual list of what lights your lights. No pun intended but you should be intentionally highlighting what specific items or housing models could give you a lifestyle you have always wanted for yourself. Remember, this is not a spoiled, selfish brat endeavor. When you are living in a home, condo or apartment suited just for you, your gifts and your talents will be able to be released enabling you to function at your highest capacity. Yes, this is for your benefit, but it is also for the benefit of all in your circle of influence. Be bold. What do you really want in your home or where do you want to live? Here's your chance to choose a coveted lifestyle that perhaps has been dormant for a very long time.

REFLECTIONS

1. What are your housing plans? Upgrade? Move? Relocate? Do Nothing? Finances don't count. Remember, you can always do something. _____

   _____

   _____

2. What are the reasons for your answer to #1? _____

   _____

   _____

3. Should you downsize and move to a new neighborhood, or renovate to prepare for retirement and or changing long term needs?

   _____

   _____

4. If you are staying put and upgrading, what areas are the most important to remodel? What will be your financial expenditure? Can you research your ROI (Return on Investment) for example, upgrading a kitchen and bathrooms? _____

   _____

   _____

CHAPTER 4

Downsize SMARTS: No One Wants Your Stuff

It's not a secret. Just look at the zillions of storage facilities cropping up all over America. You don't even want your stuff. Okay, so you have theoretically downsized, right? Do not fool yourself into believing that your move to a smaller place is all there is to understand and grasping what it means to have DESIGN SMARTS. If you are still storing possessions in a storage unit these next topics are going to change your life and save you tons of money and save you from experiencing delayed aggravation. It is time to adopt a new MINDSET (the M in SMARTS) and ask yourself these 4 essential questions:

1. Do I love it? Is it a treasure?
2. Will I ever use it?
3. Will I be excited to unpack it?
4. Or should I forget it?

This is also why I enjoy, *Love It or List It*. The show premise is completely applicable to the endless sorting activities, plus brain damaging stresses, of organizing and downsizing. Do not fall prey to the inevitable delayed aggravation by packing up your items and hauling them off to a rented storage unit having convinced yourself that you will deal with it later. This was our foolish mistake when we left our family home and moved to Cypress. Painfully of course, all those boxes haunted us years later when we finally had to deal with it all. As hard as this tedious downsizing task is, it just makes so much more sense to first go through the process of asking these soul-searching questions. And then, you will finally arrive at the true rewards of accomplishing your downsizing goals. It is not an exaggeration to say that a joyful exuberance awaits for those who persevere. This feeling of accomplishment is beyond description and definitely deserves a reward. Celebrate these life victories with perhaps a well-earned massage, a special dinner out, or finally buying those fabulous shoes. I am proud of you and I already know that your thinking cap is securely buckled, and you are ready to do battle with your own possessions. To ease up on the battle scars of sorting your possessions and deciding what to do with your no longer useful items are 3 additional suggestions.

1. Offer these items to your family or someone you know that could use it or love it.
2. Donate it to your charity of choice.
3. Or simply get rid of the guilt and just trash it.

Organizing their stuff is one of the biggest dilemmas facing homeowners. The question of where or how to start on this overwhelming exercise of downsizing can be daunting! For me personally, it was like getting a root canal. Downsizing is not one of my gifts. Many times, for me the answer was to eat that humble pie and just ask for help. There is solid wisdom in adapting the adage of only eating the elephant one bite at a time. Begin in one room. Attack one area of the room at a time—such as a closet. Set a timer to avoid becoming overwhelmed. Do not trip yourself up by putting any items back in that closet until a decision has been made! Otherwise, the same old pattern of decision-making procrastination continues. And along with that comes the self-imposed guilt that accompanies our failure to make a decision. I believe that you absolutely can succeed to win this battle of downsizing your stuff. Why? Because now you have the tools to move ahead in your personal victory!

My biggest, personal, weakness and my challenge of downsizing was my design studio which houses my design library of hundreds, if not thousands, of gorgeous fabrics. My studio is home to many accessory, furniture, lighting and kitchen and bathroom catalogs, plus stunning wallpaper books and fabric samples. In addition to this plethora of items, my multifunctional studio is where I write my blogs, create, and develop C.E.U.s (Continuing Education Units), and file all my research for my books.

So, when I pondered the question: Where do I start? The answer was crystal clear—my beloved studio. It was the most out of control and disorganized room in the house. This was a big issue for me. My growing and messy piles of disorganization were predictably compromising my productivity and peace of mind. I rationalized that my messes were due to my busy life of travel, my design business, not to mention blogging and social media demands. I repeated the paralyzing routine of putting off the inevitable job of reorganizing to another more convenient or realistic time. Of course, that time never came until Bob and I made the DESIGN SMARTS decision to relocate to another state. No amount of rationalizing or busyness could save me this time. "Do it now, Mitzi" became my call to action even though my life is even busier than before.

In order to for you to downsize differently, more intelligently, and most importantly, more effectively, your homework is to assess how pleasing or how frustrating all areas in your home are on a scale of one to ten. My studio was a definite nine. Begin preparing your MINDSET for a major overhaul, and not just rearranging things out of sight to avoid that same old pattern that got you into this conundrum in the first place. You know whom I am talking too since it takes one to know one!

The higher the frustration level, the more time is needed to realistically give your space a serious make over. On the Richter scale of frustration my design and writing studio was off the chart. Therefore, to make a major difference, in my MINDSET, I had to allocate large blocks of time plus decide that my old or irrelevant files had to be pitched, pitched, and pitched. I had first hand lived the philosophy that of the 80% that is filed, only 20% will ever be read or needed again. Ouch, this pitching of the majority of my files really hurt me because I was also, in many areas, pitching my identity of the past 30 years.

I did successfully cleanse my studio. Was it painful? Yes! I actually went through a piercingly hard and often tearful grieving process of letting most of me go. But change is often gut-wrenching. Stepping out to new levels or different lifestyles or even in many cases, a new calling is hard. Am I nervous about the new me? Absolutely I am nervous, but I am cautiously optimistic that from my personal downsizing, I am steadfastly and most assuredly moving in to my personal DESIGN SMARTS of exciting new horizons and untapped potential opportunities.

Stuff fills up storage space available!

What I mean by this statement is that if there are lots of storage spaces available to anyone in their homes, this gives the false illusion that downsizing has already happened. But in reality, things are actually stuffed behind closed closet doors or drawers. I am embarrassed to admit it, but I know how this works because Bob and I lived in this illusion for most of our married life.

As I have previously stated, there is an amazing and huge growth of storage facilities popping up everywhere today. In many cases this is not ultimately healthy to our overall well-being. Every month when we write that rental check, we are reminded of another nagging task yet to be accomplished. Beyond the emotional guilt, you may think that this is a silly overstatement until you consider these facts. First of all, storage units are not cheap. Recently there was an article about a lady moving to a smaller condominium who thought she would rent a storage unit and deal with sorting her possessions when she had the time. Her unit was only $175.00 per month so she thought no big deal since this amount would not affect her financially. However, 8 years later, she needed to move again due to changing life circumstances and she was forced to deal with the items in her storage unit.

LIFESIZING means equipping, enlightening, and empowering oneself to grab hold of life, squeezing each day's potential for a richer more fulfilling life.

No surprise actually, that when she did deal with sorting these items stored for 8 years, her conclusion was, as you might have already assumed, nothing was of any value or meaning to her at this point in her life. When she acknowledged the reality that her delayed downsizing amounted to a whopping $16,000, she was forced to admit it wasn't worth it. This decision not only cost her financially, but now it was a heavy cost to her emotionally. The consequence to her personal wellness forced her to deal with the accusing self-guilt of what she could have done with that very large sum of money. Summing up, there is always a cost associated with the procrastination of not dealing with our personal possessions. And if this cost is not yours, this ultimately will cost dearly those who eventually have to deal with all your personal possessions.

"Clutter is the result of delayed procrastination"

—Barbara Hamphill

I was very fortunate to sit next to Barbara Hamphill (Taming the Paper Tiger) during a round table discussion breakfast at a High Point Market gathering of designers. The above quote is one that Barbara is very well known for as it describes a lot of us! She is saying that our piles of paper clutter are due to not making a filing decision (procrastination) but merely putting papers in a pile to deal with later.

Now to personally connect this philosophy to our life, we know first-hand the painful delayed aggravation that follows the procrastination of making decisions on our possessions when moving time beckons. Returning to the three questions in the *Love It or Leave It* principles, we found the hardest test is the question, "Will I ever use it?" The first question of assessing "what is a treasure" was an easy decision excluding photo, personal notes and the like. Our personal debacle of 12 years ago happened during our Lifesizing event of moving from our 3500 square foot family home of thirty years, to a 1200 square foot apartment during the remodeling of our current home that we call Cypress. As defined in my previous books and work Lifesizing is a common-sense approach to experience a more fulfilling and exciting lifestyle at any age or life stage.

We totally failed at the downsizing process by the embarrassing fact that we filled up 3 entire storage units while we were remodeling. A fact that shocked us, during our year and a half of living in this small apartment, was that rarely did we miss or need something from all of our stored stuff.

Again, it was a constant reminder that we use only 20% of what we have while the other 80% takes up our valuable storage space. We had to learn the hard way to answer the gut-wrenching question and to be honest with ourselves on what is needed to truly function.

Let's recap the facts and thought-provoking points associated with the downsizing principles:

- Keep nothing out of guilt.
- Eliminating clutter from our homes makes it easier to maintain order.
- 80% of what is kept is never used.
- Stuff fills up the space available.
- Ask for help.
- Do it for your kids.
- And sorry, nobody wants most of your stuff.

Life is about living not about collecting more and more things. After all, what is obviously needed, and surely deserved, is to live with spaces that enhance and support our busy lives of today and not to be a constant source of added stress. Free yourself to live without all of your encumbering items whether it is clothes, clutter of meaningless items, or household goods never used. Your rewards will be so tangibly life-changing that you will be asking yourself why it took you so long.

Downsizing is not even close to DESIGN SMARTS

You may be thinking that this is all fine and good; but why is there all this information on downsizing if there isn't an upgrade or a relocation happening in your life? You probably already understand that disorganization, whether conscious or unconscious, blocks your peace of mind, your productivity, and obviously, visual attractiveness. However, it is unlikely you know the most destructive issue associated with those of you O50s not downsizing. It is the unfortunate fact that you will be unable to experience personally one of the primary goals of Lifesizing with DESIGN SMARTS. Downsizing involves doing, but Lifesizing with DESIGN SMARTS involves your being. Let me explain. Downsizing requires a seemingly endless amount of time sorting through boxes or closets to achieve order in your spaces. Lifesizing, on the other hand, is a new approach to your well-being by living to succeed and thrive throughout life's many transitions

As I previously stated, every stage of life demands a DESIGN SMARTS reset in order to achieve the wholeness or balance required to maneuver through each stage with grace, peace, and fulfillment of this particular time in one's life. This involves resetting ourselves with attitude adjustments, putting new boundaries in place and reaching out to others, older and wiser whom we admire and respect. Lifesizing means equipping, enlightening, and empowering oneself to grab hold of life, squeezing each day's potential for a richer more fulfilling life.

Now let's dig into this term downsizing. Most individuals perceive downsizing as having less, shedding unused items, reducing clutter, buying less, or sorting through boxes and boxes. Hearing the term downsizing is often likened to a trip to the dentist in our perception of what lies ahead moving towards tedious, soul searching cleaning out of our homes. I, for one, dread those almost torturous hours of sorting and agonizing over what to keep, donate, or trash. How then does DESIGN SMARTS give us more than merely downsizing? One word, lifestyle.

Embracing a lifestyle is vastly different than shedding material items or relocating. Downsizing is tangible and requires doing. DESIGN SMARTS result ultimately in being vs doing. Let me give you a personal example. In our home, Cypress, we experience living on a very personally fulfilling level. It is truly a joy to live with an outdoor, screened in porch, patio with fire pit, second floor balcony with a swing, beautiful sanctuary spaces throughout and rooms flooded with natural light. All of this created a new and beautiful lifestyle. Does this sound like the result of downsizing? Of course, it doesn't. This is a way of life or a lifestyle intentionally created. What is missing for most is calculating what they want their lifestyle to look like, how they want it to function. A huge obstacle that is critical to achieving their dream or vision is to identify what type of lifestyle is essential for their own specific personal fulfillment. Absolutely everyone has a unique perspective on their futures whether they think it is obtainable or simply assume that their vision can be accomplished.

Bob and I are answering these very same questions as we move to a smaller living space. On the surface, the home we bought fits all the requirements for our current life stage and Bob's retirement. No longer will outside maintenance be our responsibility. We can travel without concerns. The lovely, small community is what we sought. We're close to family and friends and are even within walking distance of shops and restaurants. Plus, the area is beautiful with tree filled rolling hills, lakes, and on and on. Ahead of us is a beautiful lifestyle that we worked very hard to find and will meet the future lifestyle we desired. We designed our lives to a new, coveted lifestyle or a new way of being for Bob and Mitzi. However, assuming we can now function in our new lifestyle, there is an entirely different scenario that requires more DESIGN SMARTS in our spaces.

In our new villa, there is lots of storage, but most is terribly nonfunctional. And I have to have privacy both inside and outside my home. That can be challenging living on a golf course. Well for those of you familiar with me and my blogs, you already know I am going to do something. First, we purchased eight-foot-tall shrubs for around the back patio. For inadequate closet space, we added more closets. My website will have photos of the before and after. The kitchen space planning is good, but it is dark with stained cabinets, mid-tone tile backsplash and stained floor. I am sure you guessed it if you've seen my Cypress home. We are planning painted white cabinets, white tile backsplash, pendant lighting, and whatever else I can figure out to brighten this very important room.

But there is so much more to determine as we make this very significant change. Where do we land for relaxing, TV or eating most of our meals? How about entertaining a friend, or many family members and dinner parties? What will be our own personal, private sanctuary spaces? What happens to our mail when we bring it in and where will we charge phones and other devices without our current mudroom? How do we control the day- to- day clutter?

> "I didn't need most of the things in storage! Although I thought I'd been tidying up, in fact, I'd been wasting my time shoving things out of sight."
>
> —Marie Kondo

For those of you wanting even more downsizing information, I have included a section from a class that I have taught on this subject. As you will see, there are repeated suggestions, but as I have stated, this is always a good thing in that repetition increases your learning. And sometimes, reading or hearing a concept in another way facilitates learning for those of us that need it.

Responses to moving or downsizing fears or excuses

One of the most difficult aspects of dealing with life stages for some individuals is the thought of actually having to move, but underneath this resistance is often the reality or the dread of downsizing years or a lifetime of stuff.

This is a list of common obstacles and suggestions for overcoming these obstacles:

- Where to begin? I tell my clients to start in one area and focus only on that area. Have 3 - 4 piles for sorting: **Keep, Give Away, Donate, Trash**
- Obviously under Give Away would be which adult children want what items so yes, piles or boxes for each adult child for them to sort through. But never take those boxes back. You have already decided to pass on those treasures!

- Hire a professional organizer, family member or trusted friend to help with this cleaning out if it is not in the homeowner's skills or motivation to do so.
- Replay success stories of others and concentrate on how freeing it was to finally be rid of all that stuff which often was only kept out of pure guilt. No one, absolutely no one has power over us but ourselves to produce or accept guilt for giving away gifts or etc.
- There are options for furniture no longer useful or needed or just not wanted any longer. Helping Hands or Habitat for Humanity, consignment shops, garage sale or even an estate sale if appropriate. Making suggestions without solutions or a plan is overwhelming.
- Some adult children don't want to see their family move or leave the home they grew up in. Downsizing can be hard on your kids too. I have heard others suggest that it's best to be firm, tell them it is your time to move but there will always be a place for them.
- Tactfully explain that the house no longer works for your needs and you are needing a less complicated lifestyle. List all your reasons: energy costs, maintenance, unused rooms etc.
- Again, reflect on the many success stories of those who have done this downsizing move will be so helpful and encouraging. Even setting up a face to face meeting with those satisfied with their moving decisions and experiences has worked wonders many, many times.
- Financially, how do I know I will not make a mistake? How did anyone predict the housing crash of this last recession? Who can predict the future? The best one can do is to calculate income versus living expenses. How do those numbers look when you evaluate staying or moving?

- Not moving can cost tons more in the long run if decisions have to made in a crisis situation such as losing a spouse, physical issues and a myriad of other life-changing surprises.
- Not wanting to give up furniture that most likely will not work in a new home. Big sigh, this is a really tough one!
- Helping my clients see a brighter, more exciting future goes a long way. Helping clients by directing their thoughts to what could be rather than cling to what is or the past can be a win-win.
- However, there are often priceless antiques or truly treasure items that are just part of who they are. If and when this is really the case, I move mountains to work those pieces into their new lifestyle. More often than not, they will eventually say, "Well, really I am so tired of that, so let's not work everything around it." But allowing them the freedom to decide this on a few items is not only honoring their past, it respects their true wishes and it is what makes them feel heard.

This additional information on downsizing may be just T.M.I. for many of you, but believe me, I have used this list many, many times to help others tackle what is normally considered one of the worst nightmares about moving. Staying put and not moving is exactly the same challenge for downsizing so hopefully, you can get inspired to just do it, like Nike says.

REFLECTIONS

1. Regardless of staying put or moving, are you downsizing your stuff? _____

   _____

   _____

2. Why or why not? _____

   _____

   _____

3. Do your closets or cabinets function for you or do they cause you frustration? If so, what changes can you make? _____

   _____

   _____

4. What design features and appliances make sense for you to upgrade? List what is not working in your current home? _____

   _____

   _____

   _____

CHAPTER 5

The O50s' Wish List

Do you remember when you were little and mom or dad or a friend asked at Christmas time, "What do you hope Santa brings you?" Well, this is an invitation for you to ponder an incredible wish list for your home life. This list is compiled from O50s, just like you that have identified their top wish lists for their homes. Can you be that little kid again and believe that your dream home can happen for you? If so, approach this chapter like it was Christmas morning.

Before I reveal the list, I want you to think about not only how you see yourself living in your future, but also where you will live. Remember, this is your dream list; dreams have no limitations. Only your own mindsets and attitudes can limit your possibilities. Therefore, shake off that old limited thinking and dream on for what could be your own fantastic life ahead.

Begin by thinking about what is working and not working for you in your current home? What do you love about your home's functionality? What are the beautiful elements that refresh you every time you enter that space? What areas drive you bonkers and make absolutely no sense? Then, ask yourself a hard question if you are married or living with someone: Where would you want to live if you were alone? Be perhaps uncharacteristically brave, ask yourself where you really would like to live and what does this look like?

DESIGN SMARTS

Since I love pondering the "what if's" because I am an untamed visionary, I am starting with my own personal short list of wanted features. This list will definitely resonate for many of my mover and shaker connections that have open mindsets to dreaming big like I do.

- Mr. Steam steam shower
- GE Monogram Advantiam oven
- Milele Combo Steam oven
- Appliance drawers, refrigerator and dishwasher
- Whole house water filtering system
- Ergonomically friendly and carefully calculated storage everywhere
- Command central combo mudroom, laundry, charging stations, lockers, etc.
- Secure dog door for beloved pets
- Screened in porch
- Advanced and controllable lighting throughout
- High tech security systems with smart home features
- "Thrive in place" features

This is the short version of my own personal top items on my wish list, but aren't they enticing to dream about? There is so much more to what the O50s are seeking, and in many cases, actually receiving. Since this powerful group is finally gaining traction in getting the building industry's attention, these and many more sought-after features, will eventually become mainstream to homeowners.

Can you imagine? Dare to dream!

There are exciting, new and innovative concepts right on the verge of happening for homeowners of today. These pioneering ideas can indeed be a reality to those creative thinkers ready to step out and step into entirely fresh and smarter living experiences.

I repurpose furniture to avoid the furniture ending up in our landfills.

Why is this happening now? It is because just like everything else throughout the O50s entire lives, this unique and often rebellious demographic has not and will not settle for the status quo in their retirement years. Research is also revealing major shifts in their likes and dislikes in the years prior to their retirement. They are demanding refined options to their pre-retirement next life stage and are saying goodbye and good riddance to those tired old homes that past generations accepted. There is a new day dawning in living arrangements for this adventurous group that will in no way reflect the norms of past generations. Here is the conceptual wish list that is exactly on point with all of DESIGN SMARTS principles.

- **Smarter designed homes** will be demanded versus merely smaller homes. The majority of this group is highly social; therefore, they need spaces to entertain in whatever fashion they choose. Adequate sizes of great rooms and indoor-outdoor entertaining areas are not simply a want but are a definite requirement.

- **Special interest rooms** are creative spaces for a myriad of uses including multi-functional activities. These accomplished homeowners will need rooms for hobbies, home offices, exercise equipment, a photography studio, and sewing or craft rooms. These spaces need to deliver more functionality than an unused and outdated bedroom supposedly redone. These rooms need to be designed with upgraded features to be a haven for personal interests, equipped with both natural and artificial lighting plus creative work spaces versus making do with an old desk. Functional storage is a no-brainer, must have feature for these special interest rooms. Flex spaces are intended to lower stress and enhance free time without the frustrations of yesterday's non-functioning storage areas. Likewise, going to a dark basement area or small room with little or no natural light will definitely not suffice for these folks. Think "she shed" or "man cave" and you get the picture!

- **Customizing is king!** No longer will shrunk-down, cookie-cutter models of former home designs be acceptable. This group believes they are individuals, one of a kind, and are exceptionally unique. Therefore, they will seek to buy home designs glorifying their specialness. As this new breed of homeowner continues to awaken their untiring demands, developers, builders, designers, and architects better take heed and get with their programs! Those in the housing industry listening will, without a doubt, be rewarded.

- **Walkable neighborhoods** score very high on the wish list for this group. Whether still working or retired, the majority of their lives have often been restricted to being indoors by geographical constraints. Add to this wanted feature is the huge amount of pet lovers, which of course translates to dog walkers, and bikers.

- **Proximity to restaurants and shopping** is certainly on this list. Remember this group is highly social, educated, and often have the finances to enjoy these amenities.

Shades of Green

But wait, there's more, lots more to this group's ideas for their wants and needs. Surprisingly, the majority of O50s are very environmentally responsible. I have a slide in my Designing and Marketing to the Boomers, a PowerPoint presentation describing the various demographics and showing a tree-hugger hippie that always gets a chuckle. But the reason for that slide is that the boomers, or the O50's way back in the 1960's, were demonstrating for environmental impact. Fast-forward to today and it is no surprise that thousands of environmentalists are the leaders in all industries as part of this age group. Transfer that philosophy to the housing industry and it gives us the green or environmentally conscious design and building processes for exterior and interior materials, finishes, and appliances the O50's place in high relevancy and esteem.

High efficiency HVAC units, upgraded insulation, tankless water heaters, energy efficient appliances and fixtures and insulated windows are just a few of those green features becoming a standard in many areas.

"Eighty percent of boomers view themselves as being basically green," says Matt Thornhill, founder and president of the Boomer Project in Richmond, Va. "And they are willing to pay more for environmentally responsible products."

My part of being green and one aspect that will be shocking!

Repeating the O50's commitment to the environment, I am sharing a few of the ways I personally try to do my part. When I left teaching to stay at home and raise my family, we made the decision to use cloth diapers. Yes, that is not a typo! The only time we used disposable diapers was for traveling. I understood the impact that all of those plastic diapers would have for generations to come in our landfills since they would never really disintegrate. Yes, I knew this would be a shocker!

This commitment was a reality even with twin babies where I credit my husband Bob for helping me every day. A big plus came at the end of the "diaper time" as these cloth diapers made the very best rags. I also made all my babies baby food because I was concerned about the quality of commercial baby food. But forgive me, I digress.

In minor ways to be green, I wash out zip lock bags for reuse, drink filtered water unless traveling to avoid contributing more water bottles to the environment, limit the amount of cleaning chemicals I use since these chemicals end up in our water supply and avoid being wasteful of food both at home and eating out (getting doggie bags).

Connecting my world of interior design to being green, I repurpose furniture to avoid the furniture ending up in our landfills. For example, the dining room table from our family home bought in 1990 is in my design studio for clients who prefer sitting at a table to bar stools at my work island. This same table will be our kitchen-eating table when we move to Ohio. There are many more examples of repurposing furniture for me personally and for my family or clients. These examples are in my videos on my website. This bunny trail, so to speak, was interjected here for the purpose of illustrating how it is possible to do these things for the good of our world.

However, my main purpose in adding this subject to this section was to underscore how the O50s do indeed care about the condition of our environment. Recognizing that there are hundreds of other ideas, this represents a very short list. Perfection Builders in Wichita uses insulated double pane glass to bring the outside in, reduce energy costs and provide substantial light. They also specify LED lighting versus incandescent bulbs which make a big difference in energy consumption. And please do not get me started on the use of fluorescent lighting for helping our environment! How many people realize these bulbs contain mercury that needs to be disposed of properly? These bulbs if discarded improperly, end up in our landfills and eventually seep mercury into our water supply.

Have I mentioned this group is social?

At the very top of any lists for this group is community. This can be family of course, but now neighborhoods designed to foster a greater sense of community are immensely popular. This is not specifically age-segregated as many of those age-segregated developments have failed due to this group's love of diversity. Nevertheless, this group, being movers and shakers, are into areas that provide opportunities to connect with others in clubhouses, heated swimming pools and fitness centers. Whether it is pickle ball courts, evening socials, clubs for different interests such as hiking, wine groups, travel groups, or whatever avenue promotes connecting one to another, they are there seeking outlets for their new-found lifestyles.

And not to be forgotten is the "lock and leave" concept due to this group's love of travel. Therefore, neighborhoods and developments that offer low maintenance exteriors plus all outdoor upkeep as part of the homeowners' association are very attractive to the O50s. If these amenities are not available, it is a little more complicated to "lock and leave". But this group is so enterprising they will figure out how to do it. But it is just more complicated. Having a neighborhood community is a huge factor assisting the "lock and leave" sought after amenity for this travel loving demographic.

Here are the top items the O50's around the country want in their homes.

DESIGN SMARTS

- **Low maintenance** everything goes without saying if you know anything about this demographic. Spending their weekends doing chores and home projects is a thing of their past that they are more than ready and happy to give up so they can now enjoy their time. Maintenance free means no yard work, painting outside, snow removal, leaf clean up, grass cutting or hedge trimming. In general, all outside is someone else's responsibility. Imagine that scenario!

- **One floor living** is also an overwhelming must have for many O50s, but not for everyone. Having a loft is desirable as a flex space or to accommodate those extra, but infrequent, guests. However, wanting a first floor only space is often due to mobility issues. This will be thoroughly covered in Chapter 7: Healthy Home = Healthy Life.

- **High technology home systems** now do more than ever. This has just begun to emerge as a must for the O50s. Remotes, keypads, smartphones, or tablets can control or monitor lights, sound systems, temperature control, alarms, sprinkler systems, window treatments and medical information. For example, there is now even a toilet that can monitor your blood sugar levels.

- **Laundry mudrooms** can be designed to be a multitask command-like home center with charging stations, counter space for work, hobbies, pet washing, household storage, and oh yes, even laundry.

- **Master suites** that include two sleeping rooms each with their own bathroom essentials, such as a water closet and sink, and a shared shower, tub, and common sitting area for reading, TV, or personal sanctuary spaces.

- **Updated garages** will become safer with zero-clearance home entrances or improved entrances with good lighting, handrails, and shelving or cabinets by entrance doors for groceries, etc.

- **Kitchens** will continue to evolve into the center or heart of the home. They can have user-friendly ergonomic appliances, cabinetry, under-counter lighting, refrigerator, freezer, dishwasher drawers, easy care everything, pullout drawers versus doored cabinets, and islands. These amenities will become ultra-important for work, socializing, casual dining, serving, and oh yes, even cooking prep.

And yes, there's tons more ahead!

Watch for innovative open space design that brings the outdoors inside. Research and trend watchers report that more visual exterior viewing is not only desired, but it is good for our health by creating calm through experiencing nature.

- **Easy-care everything**, including flooring materials, furniture, counters, etc.

- **Private Outdoor patio** with optional gardening space. The key word here is PRIVATE.

- **Outdoor kitchens** are becoming increasingly common place. Since this O50 group loves their outdoor living, it only stands to reason that cooking outdoors will gain in popularity.

- **Entertaining spaces** will be very important and will have storage for functional equipment and serving. These spaces will also require multi-task furniture to serve as work or entertaining areas, as in more casual tables and seating that also can serve Thanksgiving dinner using Grandma's china.

- **Open-space designed homes** will be reevaluated to include multitasking activities like computer work areas along with TV viewing for family and guests.

- **Personal sanctuary spaces** will be common as the O50's lives continue to be or will get busier whether they are retired or not.

- **Upgraded lighting and lighting systems** will become the norm, especially among single women, for security inside and out.

- **"Storage, storage, storage"** is the common cry; even though downsizing, they want what they want where they want it.

- **Luxury bathroom items** like steam showers, heated tile flooring, large sauna-type showers and therapeutic bathtubs to soothe all aches and pains away. It is not simply a Jacuzzi tub. TV and sound systems, cabinetry with drawers for easy use, luxury tiles and counter materials and high-end fixtures are desired. Finally, upgraded lighting is needed everywhere, including sensors to turn on and off during those nighttime trips to the bathroom.

Can you believe?

Wouldn't it be exciting to live in these spaces? These features are becoming more and more prevalent, making them a lovely reality. First for you however, is developing a new MINDSET on defining priorities for these sought-after features? What has historically occurred is that builders decide what design features they will offer. Therefore, homeowners were forced to adjust and fit into their home's design and lifestyle accordingly.

In order to have a fresh and exciting DESIGN SMARTS driven and designed home, the homeowner must be in charge to decide what they want, and not merely accept what is available to them.

In the kindest way it can be stated, something can always be done!

But you're probably saying, "Oh sure, easy for you to say when you are not paying for all these fabulous features." Oh, but I am thinking of the costs. What I have observed, in over thirty years of working with homeowners in my interior design business is that, to put it bluntly, more times than not I am trying to salvage the homeowners project resulting from badly designed homes. Of course, there are some exceptions, but overall, homeowners are paying for various options supplied by builders that are really not important to them. More importantly, they never asked for them in the first place. A high percentage of the financial costs in the construction of our homes include items no longer desired or rooms no longer utilized.

By truly evaluating exactly what is important and eliminating those items that are not wanted or needed, these exciting updated features can indeed be affordable. Instead of taking a "pot of money" and distributing it throughout the entire home, allocate the same budgeted amount of money for the features truly wanted and needed. The same amount of money is spent, but now is spent on items and rooms that are for the O50s of today and not on those same old, tired floor plans and options of the past.

It is essential to connect the dots of the DESIGN SMARTS philosophy in contemplating a fresh, new, and innovative future lifestyle. The premise we embraced in creating the original Lifesizing principles, emphasized that mindsets and attitudes are the keys to living a life that is overflowing with vibrant, fresh, and exciting experiences. Absolutely nothing will ever change without the choice to make changes, whether personally, or in the home.

Therefore, can you dare to dream without limits, believe in possibilities, and be fiercely determined to choose what your life could contain for you and those you love and care for in your world? If your answer is yes, your life can potentially be full of Christmas morning joy as you position yourself to receive your most sought-after gift, a life resulting from calculated choice, not a life of haphazard chance.

> "Imagination is more important than knowledge.
> Knowledge is limited. Imagination encircles the world"
>
> —Albert Einstein

REFLECTIONS

Your Dream List

> "Dwell in possibility."
>
> ~ Emily Dickinson

Can you dare to dream without limitations? What features or fixtures would you love to have in your home? _____

_____

_____

_____

Do you believe in living a green lifestyle?" If so, what are the ways you are green in your home? _____

_____

_____

_____

CHAPTER 6

Does Your Home Have A Soul?

> "Downsize your beliefs that your home is merely that, your home. There is so much more that your home can give to you."
>
> —Mitzi Beach

When you walk over the threshold into your home from the garage, can you feel the barrier from the frenzied, noisy, busy world you left behind as the garage door closes? Is there a welcome relief and familiar sense of security and warmth enveloping you like putting on your favorite robe and stepping into your comfy slippers? Don't you want return to your beloved home and unwind? Finally breathe a cleansing sigh of relief, and embrace the calming, underlying message that comes from a beautiful, peaceful, and ordered space?

I strongly believe that the emotions that either assault or welcome you as you walk through your front door or from your garage, sets the tone for what happens next in your life. These tangible emotions will either be beckoning you to continue the nerve-racking stresses of your day or enable you to cast them off to deal with them another time. Yes, an emphatic yes, is the immense exponential power your spaces have on impacting your life in untold ways.

However, for me personally, with feedback from clients and family, until the changes are made, you will forfeit your potential "Ahh, finally, I'm home" experience.

I have heard dozens, maybe hundreds of times over my 30-year design career what a difference intentional design upgrades have made in my client's lives. Nothing gives me greater joy than to see the faces of satisfied homeowners who exchanged the old way for a new, better, upgraded way. What you think is normal and inevitable isn't always so. for them what these made in exchange for what they formerly had accepted as their normal home life. And yet, there still remain those stubborn naysayers that refute the substantial emotional impact, whether it is a negative or a positive influence that homes have on daily lives.

Vast amounts of research, along with my own design knowledge and experience, verify this philosophy that spaces are either working for us or are working against us.

Some of my toughest, most strong-willed clients even had to admit that they had no idea how much better they felt after simply replacing those horrid, fluorescent light fixtures with a kinder, softer option for their lighting. And this was merely their lighting so imagine the response after doing some major upgrades? Do not fall into the trap of doing nothing because you believe the costs are impossible. In the kindest way it can be stated—something can always be done!

This is exactly why, way back in the early 2000's I coined the term Lifesizing. In reviewing my design files for this book, I came across my hand-written index card from 2002 that says:

> "I strongly believe that our spaces affect our relationships, our productivity and our overall sense of well-being. As we seek to remodel our spaces, our lives will invariably be remodeled as well."
>
> —Mitzi Beach

My first thought after I found the card (and stopped laughing) was, *very impressive Mitzi*! But seriously, I am not sure why I had this passion over 15 years ago, but intuitively I knew to trademark Lifesizing®. This same passion has evolved into DESIGN SMARTS—design tools to equip and to establish the critical boundaries between home and the stressful outside world.

Space is never silent

Folks are always telling Bob and I how peaceful and safe our home feels. You must know by now, this is not a fluke nor by accident. DESIGN SMARTS represent the intentional application of the Lifesizing® principles that were carefully and intentionally designed into our home, Cypress.

This is my lifetime passion. I sincerely want all of you to grasp these tangible and intangible life-giving, spirit-enriching DESIGN SMARTS concepts. If you are like many of us, you are stunned at how quickly time is zooming by. But I urge you to grasp the reality that you can do more with your life and your time. It's not too late. By incorporating these DESIGN SMARTS basics, starting with your home, exhilarating and beautiful happenings await you and those you love.

What greets you when you enter your home?

When you return to your home, most likely you are entering from your garage into your laundry area or another typically over-looked space. Because this is your normal routine, the odds are that not much thought is given to this space, right? But for the majority of homeowners, whether it is a condo, apartment or loft, there is an unconscious reaction in your emotion meter. Regardless, if you consciously or unconsciously register any emotion at all, there is unquestionably, a reaction. It is irrelevant if you are aware or not, it is there in a vast number of ways assaulting you or welcoming you home. And perhaps the saddest of all these unchecked emotional effects, is what your unconscious stress is doing to you, your spouse or your family. It's the constant pitfall of waiting for the other shoe to drop when a home's neglected; annoying spaces can set off emotional time. Exaggeration? The dog has had disgusting, yucky accidents, the phone is ringing, you are tired, cranky, and hungry and you have no idea what to have for dinner.

You know exactly what this means personally, or you have witnessed this in your family's homes. If there are piles of laundry, kitchen counters over-flowing with mail, laptops, purses and cell phones, already the stage is set for a stressful overload of what is next even before life happens, like moody kids or out of sorts spouses.

But take heart!

There's a myriad of doable and definitely cost-effective ways to diffuse these debilitating areas in your home. Let me count those ways starting with your lighting. Is it cold and glaring from a functional but non-friendly fluorescent light fixture or depressingly dim light? Is the laundry piled up? Do you see an endless river of clutter? Messy pet dishes, a non-descript paint color on the walls, and even overflowing trash bins?

If so, you most assuredly are not alone! But are these issues really a big deal or just part of everyday living? They definitely are a big deal to your well-being and your answer will tell you how aware you are of the impact of your spaces.

I continually observed homeowners manipulating themselves to adjust to their current home space rather than doing what is needed to manipulate their homes to meet their needs instead

If you are like most people, your mind is running full tilt: What is next on your schedule? What is for dinner? Who has to be where? And how much time is there to do all the things that need to be done? Now, imagine returning home and how you would feel with an uncluttered counter for your purse, laptop, mail, even packages while your mind settles in for what is next to do. You could experience soothing, gentle, but sufficient lighting, a clear pathway from the garage or your front door with an interesting or fun runner; the walls have your favorite color or even wallpaper, along with a fun poster or art work. Yes, these design upgrades are a game changer. The result is more than a pretty space. This is a difference that positively affects your moods, your energy, but most importantly, lowers your stress. The enormous popularity of home lockers today proves even further the overdue awakening for needed solutions to conquering the stresses of everyday life caused by poorly designed spaces.

Design changes lives

Yes, without a doubt, design changes lives. With decades of experience designing for clients and family, I have witnessed first-hand how intentional and specifically calculated design improvements positively affect lives, especially in rectifying those every day nagging problem areas. For example, a working mom's newly designed storage spaces at the back-door area made a huge difference in ending her normal daily frustration of unrelenting piles of "stuff" on the kitchen island or counters. The emotional onslaught of a messy, unorganized kitchen is what she previously had to overcome before she could even begin to think about getting dinner or starting her evening. But now, after her intentional reorganization of her former debilitating and out of control laundry room, she's mentally empowered to calmly address her next demand. It is unarguably life changing how the impact of functional design affects our lives.

Form follows function

If you could only hear how clients or family excitedly respond to simply rearranging furniture or adding lighting, you would agree that living spaces intentionally designed, absolutely affect the quality of our lives both unconsciously and consciously. Often, the unexpected outcome of upgraded space is a new, more positive outlook on life. This is because beautiful and functional spaces elevate all our senses to be and do more with time spent in spaces that inspires us, not hinder us. Vast amounts of research, along with my own design knowledge and experience, verify this philosophy that spaces are either working for us or are working against us.

This is why I boldly profess that space is never silent. There is always a message sent out from any given space. Recently, I was in a doctor's waiting room of super-bright glaring lighting, industrial grey looking carpeting, navy chairs, non-descript mauve-like wall paint, and cheap orange oak end tables cluttered with outdated magazines. Would you believe this horrible waiting room was for women? For heavens sakes, bad design choices are rampant. I say choices because someone had to have chosen these awful combinations of finishing selections.

For the same pricing, a fresh wall paint of light peach, apple green and cobalt blue fabrics and accents, LED ceiling lighting in the 2700 range, and dark stained end tables would have made us women feel more relaxed and less stressed in this awful dark and depressing waiting room. It's always a matter of finish selections by someone who understands who will be in any particular space that will make or break the message given in homes or offices.

Space is never benign!

Dr. Shilagh Mirgain's article, "*The Connection between Your Home and Your Sense of Well Being*" is timely and relevant, supporting information on this subject of home's special impact. She states, "Your home and work environment are an important influence on your sense of well-being, but they are often overlooked. These are the environments we spend the most time in, so it's only natural they would have an impact on us."

Is your home actually "Home Sweet Home" to you? Again, ask yourself the question, what message either greets you or assaults you as you come home? In the modern fast paced world, of today, your living spaces can provide a nurturing, restorative, safe, comfortable place to refuel, relax, and recover from our complicated and busy lives. Sadly, the opposite is true. Your home can unconsciously add to the stress of daily living by being cluttered, disorganized, nonfunctional, uninviting, cold or depressing and basically just a place to land and exist. But take heart if this is your home! Change can assuredly happen as you read on for every day solutions to common issues in the homes of today.

Spaces not only have the capability to influence us in a positive manner, but our spaces can definitely have a negative influence on our emotional health and physical well-being. The American Society of Interior Designers (A.S.I.D.), along with other respected interior design and architectural organizations, have invested years of research evaluating the outcomes of environmental changes in schools, offices, health care, and now, finally, our homes. Research now proves that color, lighting, natural lighting, indoor plants, noise reduction, privacy features, and ergonomics play an integral role in our state of well-being in our interior spaces.

Knowledge is always the key to moving forward in any endeavor. Knowledge empowers. By learning the basic design principles in this book, you will be equipped to be your own "space doctor". With an unbiased eye, you will be able to diagnosis what is wrong by critically examining each of your spaces and ask yourself what you like and what is not working for you. The good news is that you can always transform your own spaces by doing something. You know the famous Nike add, "Just do it". Many times, homeowners find that hiring a professional interior designer, a home organizer, or one of the many fields that specialize in assisting homeowners today, is well worth the cost to make a significant and life changing difference.

Over the decades of working with clients, I continually observed homeowners manipulating themselves to adjust to their current home space rather than doing what is needed to manipulate their homes to meet their needs. This is exactly what I was unsuccessfully trying to do in our previous family home of 30 years that had outlived its usefulness when we became empty nesters. Therefore, in my own personal dilemma, I said to myself, "Life is short and getting shorter as the years go flying by. Let's get out of this home, with these negative influencing spaces that do not work anymore, and into ones that will work for us now and in the future. And that is exactly what transpired during the buying, re-designing, and restoration of Cypress.

The question that begs to be asked is: "How are you actually living in your home's spaces?" I must repeat again the fascinating statistic for most homeowners is realizing that 80% of the time is actually spent in only 20% of the home's spaces? This is normally a huge surprise to most people and an incredibly profound fact as people begin to see it to be true in daily living patterns. Track this statement for yourself and see if this doesn't relate to your most frequently used hang out spaces regardless if you are in a 5000 square ft or 1800 square foot home, apartment, or condo.

The next questions that beg to be asked are: "What do those 20% of your home's spaces look like? Do they nurture you? Do they have comfortable furniture and good lighting? Is there a convenient table nearby? Is it conducive to your multitasking functions?" Of all the changes you can make in your home, upgrading where you spend most of your life certainly necessitates whatever effort is required. The time and attention given to your 80% space will reap vast rewards in personal benefits many times over.

Where is your place to get your home hugs?

What a smart investment it is then to invest the time to make the most of your time in your home by providing priceless pay backs year after year. It is essential to have the most comfortable and good quality furniture where you live most of your time versus those rooms rarely used! The best lighting should be there also. This space, where you spend 80% of your home life, should be a delightfully nurturing, comfortable, space filled with your favorite treasures and definitely free of clutter and disorganization. With the exception of the kitchen or bathroom, your 80%-time segment spent in 20% of your home is indeed the most important space because this is really where your life happens! This sounds like an obvious occurrence for most homes, right? Wrong! It's shocking to actually observe how many smart people spend a majority of their life in compromised, depressing rooms.

Priority must reign here in the effort spent to accomplish lovely, specifically functioning rooms that give limitless needed nurturing and appreciated restoration. Who doesn't need or benefit from rooms like these? I want these rooms for you!

If you are ready to take action and make a difference in your home for yourself and your loved ones, these DESIGN SMARTS principles will undoubtedly facilitate your attempts to achieve your goals to have the home you have always wanted for yourself and those you care about when they are in your home.

Action Steps

1. Control the clutter since it adversely affects the peace of your home. Well-organized and uncluttered spaces can also directly affect the safety of your home as well as providing a calming ambiance so appreciated in these unusually stressful times.

2. Evaluate your lighting and then upgrade it. You will be amazed at the wonderful difference. Better lighting not only positively influences your moods, but a higher level of appropriate lighting increases your home's functionality. Better lighting is known to reduce nagging eye strain that can contribute to more stress and fatigue when trying to achieve any activity in a poorly lit space. There is much more ahead to cover with lighting, especially for the safety aspects directly related to lighting.

3. Also, evaluate your stuff. Keep nothing out of guilt. Embrace the "less is more" philosophy to achieve organization, function, and ease of any home activity.

4. Create personal sanctuary spaces for everyone living in your home. It is possible and it is the means to establishing personal fulfillment and restful resets to face another day.

5. Control sound and privacy in designing your spaces. Noise is a stressor that must be acknowledged for its compromising negative effects.

6. Comfort is king in furniture, space planning, materials and finishes. Choose wisely in all categories. Books are written on these topics; but suffice it to say any facet of your home needs comfort to reign over looks. Comfort and beauty in rooms is not an oxymoron because I have done it for myself and many of my clients and friends.

"Our homes should be filled with light and love. Without both, the home is soul-less"

—Mitzi Beach

 **REFLECTIONS**

What action steps will you take to create a restorative, nurturing environment in your home? _____

_____

_____

_____

_____

_____

_____

_____

_____

CHAPTER 7

Healthy Home = Healthy Life

Is your home a healthy home? Not sure? Answer these questions and find out.

- If you had a cast, or recent surgery, or a recent knee or hip replacement, what bathroom in your current home would work for you to easily take a shower?

- Do you even have a first-floor bathroom where you can maneuver safely and easily for your basic needs if you are on crutches from a procedure or accident?

- Do you have your own private, personal sanctuary space in your current home? What could a sanctuary space possibly have anything to do with a healthy home?

- When entering or leaving your home through your garage, is there a landing, with wide, deep steps, good lighting, and a handrail?

- When working in your kitchen, are you constantly reaching up or bending down to do everyday tasks?

Your answers to these questions will reveal whether you are living in a healthy home that daily equips and empowers you to live a healthier life. Or are you living in one that constantly compromises your wellbeing and wellness? If there is any chapter in this book that resonates and motivates you to change your present wellness status, this is the one! One last question, do you think this chapter is only for those in an older category than you are? If so, please read this true story.

I know this is a true story because it happened to my son when he was 35 years old, married with 3 children under the age of five, including a 9-month-old baby. As with most life changing crises, he and his wife's life changed in an instant! Due to a very serious accident requiring numerous leg surgeries and months of recovery time, he was forced to live on the first floor of their home. Because they lived in a typical two-story home with all of the bedrooms and bathrooms located upstairs, major home adjustments had to be made immediately to accommodate my son's inability to navigate up the stairs. His twin brother was a God send removing all their dining room furniture and setting up a bed, a TV, work space, and basic amenities in the dining room to survive all the pain and months of therapy. The first-floor powder room in this older home was typically tiny with a narrow door and barely enough room to turn around with full mobility. I was incredibly impressed at the family's endurance. But obviously, this life changing event took its toll on every one of them.

There are two obvious points to make in this true-life example. The first one is that accidents or surgeries happen at all ages and not just for those over 65. The second point is a healthy home makes life healthier for all ages. Observing young families schlepping endless amounts of baby equipment up and down entry stairs or trying to potty train a toddler in a tiny powder room, exemplifies the need for not only smarter designed homes, but healthier homes as well.

Why is wellness the buzz seemingly everywhere today? It is difficult to escape the plethora of health and wellness topics dominant throughout all types of media outlets including TV, newspapers, social media, and the internet. This major wellness phenomenon as predicted has finally trickled down to the housing industry. However, this has mostly occurred due to savvy consumers demand for smarter designed homes and smarter designed products.

Recently, The Wall Street Journal's weekend section, OFF DUTY[1], highlighted this growing trend of incorporating safety in our homes. As stated in the article, "Talk about modifying a home for "aging in place" and baby boomers recoil, in fear of mortality and worse, ugliness. Now the design industry is filling this niche, stylishly". The article goes on to dismiss concerns that safety features will be diminishing the value of homes. "Design for aging in place actually entices some buyers," said Diane Harris, former editor in chief of Money magazine and currently the editorial director of Considerable, a financial and lifestyle brand targeting people in their 50s and 60s. "A first-floor bathroom that includes a shower adds more flexibility to a house layout," she said. "A first-floor laundry room is great for seniors -- and also a young family".

This newspaper article goes on to relay the story of a 60-year-old lady who is an active tennis player and a client of designer Michael A. Thomas, a Certified Aging in Place Specialist, (CAPS). She balked at his suggestion of incorporating safety features in her bathroom believing that any modifications would make her appear "old". Mr. Thomas did finally persuade her in taking his expert advice. Six months later, she shattered both of her knees on the tennis court. Because her remodeled bathroom could accommodate her recovery needs, she was able to return home instead of spending weeks in a rehab center.

Yes, the times certainly are changing in homeowner's perceptions regarding preparing their homes to be more convenient, ergonomic, and safe. When our home was recently one of four homes on a symphony fund raising home tour, our local newspaper promoted the event by featuring our home as an aging in place home. Five hundred people toured our home in 2 days. Half of them or more were curious to see what an aging in place home actually looked like. Our favorite comment, of course, was that our home was beautiful. But unless pointed out, they had no idea of our aging in place features. Needless to say, there were many converted believers after seeing first-hand how a smarter and healthier design could seamlessly fit into any home and it didn't have a "medical" or "old" stigma.

DESIGN SMARTS check list for healthier homes

1. **Walk-in or curb-free shower.** While also making the bathroom look modern and sophisticated, this also eliminates a major tripping hazard by designing a shower base with no tile curb to step over when getting in and out of the shower. An acquaintance of mine, an active early 60-year-old, tripped over the tile curb getting in to her very high-end bathroom shower. After months of unsuccessful physical therapy, she endured a life changing knee replacement, all from a healthy woman tripping in her own bathroom!

2. **Smart shower features** include a rain head shower fixture with a free hand-held shower sprayer with attached grab bars by a shower seat. It should also include at least one grab bar and non-slip shower floor. These will exponentially increase shower safety.

3. **Bath tubs with a generous side** deck (6" or more) without a doubt, makes it easier to get in and out of the bathtub.

4. **Below counter kitchen drawers** are super smart versus upper cabinets or what I call, doored boxes on the wall. Below counter, doored cabinets, even with pull outs, require constant bending

which is why drawers are ergonomically superior for storage within easy reach.

5. **Appliance drawers** which help people avoid straining are the new must haves by bringing items closer. Major new options are quickly becoming the kitchen darlings like microwave drawers, dishwasher drawers, refrigerator and freezer drawers.

6. **Comfort height or "Right Height" toilets** are so popular now that they are almost becoming a standard selection for homeowners unless a children's wing is necessary.

7. **Wide doorways,** at least 32 inches wide, allow for greater accessibility plus also gives the impression of more spaciousness in the home.

8. **Lever-style doorknobs** and lever style kitchen and shower faucets are easy to operate especially when carrying items.

In addition to this check list, it goes without saying that a one floor home that includes an almost level or no step entry from the garage remains the ultimate goal for any of the O50s regardless of geographical location. The challenge facing many, if living in very expensive areas, is that land is a premium cost factor making one floor living an unrealistic goal. In the next chapter titled *The Housing Revolution is Upon Us*, exciting new models of living are bursting out all over our country. But first, there are more items to consider for DESIGN SMARTS features.

A COMMON-SENSE checklist for healthier homes that isn't so common

This list may contain a few repeats. But being a firm believer that repetition enhances learning, this is strictly by intention.

- Contrasting color for bottom steps versus floor areas where tripping could be an issue.
- Slip-resistant bathroom surfaces.
- Additional lighting everywhere.
- Laundry on the first floor by the master bedroom, or an upstairs laundry space.
- A minimal number of throw rugs and area rugs; use double-sided tape if you have them to stabilize.
- A master and a full bath on the first floor or dedicated spacing in a two-story house to accommodate an elevator if needed.
- Doors with 32- to 36-inch clear openings to accommodate walkers, wheelchairs and strollers, luggage, and even groceries
- Handrails on both sides of stairways.
- Appliances and cabinetry to meet ergonomic conveniences.
- Different heights for kitchen counters.
- Short-pile carpeting or hard-surface flooring
- Lever door and fixture handles (instead of twist knobs).
- Comfort-height toilets and grab bars in bathrooms.
- Zero clearance or no curb for shower.
- Eliminate shower/tub combinations for master bath.
- Showers with a sit-down bench and hand-held shower sprayer; a second shower head option.
- Garage entry to house with handrail, landing and lighting.
- Less furniture and traffic patterns free from clutter.
- Efficient storage spaces, even in garages
- Windows that open easily.
- Bigger bathrooms.
- Energy efficient HVAC systems and appliances.
- Security Systems and Smart Home Technology systems.

When we bought our extremely, run-down 1930's home, we knew that our restoration project would be that type of undertaking that most people would consider crazy and that we had lost of ever-loving minds and we were right, they did!

However, I had previously become CAPS certified, or a Certified Aging in Place Specialist, which influenced all aspects of my own personal design project to incorporate the SMARTS DESIGN principles, specifically the SPACE factors critically essential to achieve a healthy home. A short list of aging in place elements for safety and comfort that we incorporated into our restored home includes a no-step entry from the garage, a dedicated space for an elevator if needed, 36" wide doorways, upgraded lighting, wide hallways and stairways, an open, uncluttered floor plan, comfort height toilets, handrails in the bathrooms, ergonomic kitchen appliances as well as ergonomic dedicated storage, slip resistant flooring throughout the entire home, easy maintenance finishes, and a barrier free bathroom and bedroom on the first floor.

Needless to say, our years of living Cypress, have not only given us a dreamy lifestyle, but this home promoted our health and well-being in our physical safety and consequently in our emotional wellbeing by the security of experiencing how tangibly safe we were. Some of our intentional design features were obvious while other features were stealthier. These additional, healthy home features may or may not be visibly prominent but there is absolutely no doubt, they matter!

1. De-Clutter! Not only for visual peace of mind, clutter is a major cause for falls and accidents. Examples of accident producing clutter are in the laundry/garage traffic pattern areas and of course, clutter on any stairs.

2. Change light switches to easy to operate rocker type light switches.

3. Add lighting! At 50 years of age, 40% less light is received in our corneas. Most homes rarely upgrade the lighting, making accidents easier to happen simply due to poor lighting, not to mention the unconscious stress caused by poor lighting.

4. Ditch the throw rugs! Pick up those throw rugs in traffic areas or any throw rugs without a non-slip backing.

5. Add a handrail, a larger landing area, and improve lighting to the garage entrance in the home.

6. Get rid of all electrical cords that could be tripped over or are hanging from desks or islands. There are many alternatives now to alleviate this hazard.

7. Evaluate how much furniture you have in your rooms that could prevent easy accessibility; less is more for healthy homes.

8. Add handrails in bathtubs and showers. Today, there are many options that do not have to be installed during construction but can be added later if planned for.

9. Add sensor night-lighting from bedroom to bathroom traffic patterns for nighttime trips that often end in a fall without adequate lighting.

There is one final question to ask in closing this chapter on healthy homes which is: "What good is a robust healthy lifestyle if you are living in a home lurking with accident prone features"? Cited in these chapters are real life stories describing life changing accidents. What is not included are the untold number of home accidents I could relay to you, but enough is enough already. I must confess, though, that whenever I observe someone with a cast or on scooter with a boot or cast, I have to ask myself: "What was the cause?" Even I am shocked to hear over and over the report of how it happened in their own homes! Therefore, let's do this healthy home endeavor together, encouraging others by sharing these lists or verbally motivating your circle of influence. I personally think sharing these features with others would be a beautiful and long-lasting gift for you to show how much you care about their safety too.

> "A house is built by wisdom and becomes strong through good sense. Through knowledge, its rooms are filled with all sorts of precious riches and valuables."
>
> —Proverbs 24:3

Now that you are qualified as a DESIGN SMARTS expert, list the areas in your current home that definitely could use a dose of healthy helps. Please be brutally honest. Your list of your own home's area needing safety upgrades is to be proactive for the sole purpose of your own personal wellness safety, not for anyone else to judge or debate its value. Your safety is highly valuable! Just ask anyone dealing with the consequences of either home accidents or the inadequacies of their homes after a medical procedure or accident of any kind.

CHAPTER 8

The Housing Revolution Is Upon Us

The American dream of owning the typical home, I believe, has died a slow and painful death. Yes, you read this correctly. I am pronouncing death to what we have come to accept as standard housing in America due to ignoring the following:

- The financial reality of millions in America today.
- Millions of hard-working people have never recovered financially from the devastating effects of the 2008 recession.
- Statistics predict that, by the year 2030, over half of Americans will be over 50 years old. The aging of America in relevant housing models is nearing the crisis stage.
- The new wave of living to experience life with simpler housing, versus seeking status and success by where or how one lives, is having a profound effect on the American Housing Industry.
- Currently, only 20% of millennials are making over $100,000 yearly, resulting in their limited housing opportunities. Is living with their parents their only option?
- Boomers are spending billions of dollars supporting their grown children. What are the options for those Gen Y or Gen X kids that do not have parental financial support?

- Single parents? Single women? Widows and widowers? Many of the millions that fall into these categories are living a desperately meager life of simply trying to survive. What are their realistic housing options?

I am in no way advocating for government- subsidized housing. However, I am imploring the movers and shakers of the building and design industry to ignite their creativity and commence developing exciting new and relevant housing options needed for our changing demographic profile in America today. I have been calling for this overdue change that is needed in our housing industry, a housing revolution, for over a decade. Therefore, I am definitely not surprised in the least at all of the variations of home styles developing. What certainly does surprise me is that this housing revolution has taken so long to develop. I have frequently compared re-inventing the housing industry in America to trying to move a cruise ship with an oar.

As previously highlighted in these chapters, the American landscape of demographics has drastically changed over the last few decades. And yet, surprisingly, we are just now seeing this housing revolution evolve. Where and why did the burgeoning phenomenon of the unexpected tiny home movement emerge from today? It is happening because hundreds of thousands of Americans are desperately seeking housing that works for their needs; that is the reason.

Fallout from the demise of the extended family

I grew up in NE Ohio with grandparents, aunts and uncles, and a plethora of cousins. Amazingly, I still remember when, at 5 years old, I had my tonsils removed. I stayed at my Aunt Bea and Uncle Al's house because my mom was a working mom. This was not an uncommon super generous act on my aunt and uncle's part. No, it was just the normal way families took care of each other in those days. I also distinctly remember my mom and dad taking care of our elderly Great Aunt Susie and Uncle Martin by taking them food, checking on them and including them for dinners and family events.

Many of you readers probably already know that Bob and I are the oldest on the leading edge of the baby boomers; or those born between 1946 and 1964. What you may not know is that we were also part of the beginning of another huge movement in American. The huge O50 generation began to move away from their extended families for new career opportunities and other reasons. Of course, people were doing this in other time periods, but not in the great numbers seen in the late 1960's and 1970's.

Perhaps a personal bunny trail here, but I clearly remember, after graduating from Ohio University, getting married, leaving my small, close-knit family and moving to New Jersey. Bob was starting his career with a large oil company as an engineer in oil refineries. Bob grew up in a military family. Moving away from family was common for him, but certainly not for me. Although I was a new bride, I was lonely, miserable, and homesick. I didn't know anyone close who could help me learn how to do married life? When I was so sick from being pregnant with twins, I ended up in the hospital for hydration IVs. Who was there to help me? Basically, it was Bob and me trying to make it all work. The friends that we had made were all working or busy with their own small families. I have shared this personal life experience to illustrate the challenges facing millions if they are living without a caring family or a reliable community for support.

Why or how does my personal history relate to America's housing crisis and the need for a housing revolution? The main reasons are the financial implications of living without a support system of a family or community. I am not addressing the substantial, adverse, sociological realities of the breakup of the extended family in this chapter on housing.

If you were suddenly divorced, and I say suddenly, because for many this is not a planned event in our current culture and you were living in a 4- bedroom home, how would you take care of your home? Would you want to continue living in the home that constantly reminded you of the painful reality of unexpectantly being forced into singlehood? And if you decide to move, where would you go and what type of housing would you want, or could you afford?

A U.S. Census Bureau report, released August 27, 2013, revealed that the traditional American household of a married couple with children is quickly becoming a minority versus formerly being a majority of home ownership. I thought that this was a startling fact until further being shocked that married couples with children shrunk by half between 1970 and 2012. Another significant statistic is the number of single Americans living alone has risen from 17% to 27% and no doubt that number is substantially higher today. Now, I am not a mathematical genius, but this census revelation tells us that over one-quarter of Americans are single and are living alone.

Another trend that was equally shocking to me is the number of Boomers, or the O50s, moving in with their parents! Regardless of their education or professional career, when an unexpected life crisis hits them, moving in with their aging parents is their only option. The question that begs to be asked is, "How do individuals representing these startling statistics fit into the typical American home?" The answer is obvious; they do not fit into our current home models of today. This is why so many millions of Americans are now, by necessity, living in the ill-suited, typical American home styles.

Over 60 million Americans live in multi-generational housing

Shifting demographics has created an explosion of multi-generational, or lifetime homes. If we face the facts, we are in a glass bubble of denial that is about to shatter. Fortunate are the ones that have planned for this type of living arrangement. But even if moving in with one's mother-in-law, elderly parent, or single parent with children is an expected change, basic remodeling is imperative to provide the privacy and adequate lifestyle maintenance for all living in their new lifestyle home. For example, when my daughter and her husband moved his mother into their home, adjustments had to be made. Remodeling made it necessary to add an office with an attached bathroom because they graciously gave up one of the bedrooms which was formerly a home office.

Multi-generational homes will often house all ages. Therefore, installing basic aging in place elements are immensely important features, especially for the bathroom. It is no surprise that insurance data tells us that the bathroom is the most dangerous area in the home. Mostly due to inadequate safety features, every 18 seconds someone over 65 years of age falls in their bathroom. DESIGN SMARTS urges separate tub and shower facilities to help prevent serious bathroom falls. Therefore, if at all possible, avoid the bathtub/shower combo.

Features of the ultimate independent living suite

- Private entrance
- Private bathroom
- Private bedroom
- Eat in kitchenette
- Living room
- Laundry

To many homeowners this sounds terribly unrealistic and very costly. However, so often homeowners conclude they could not possibly afford to remodel their existing home to integrate an independent living suite. The expense seems high until the reality of housing a family member outside the home is calculated. One month in assisted living is a minimum of $5000.00 with a yearly minimum amount of $60,000.00 which adds up to an enormous sum in a very short time. Compared to a year's assisted living cost, an independent living suite is a bargain. And there are additional considerations of incorporating a lifetime suite into your house for a perfectly healthy family member for the sole purpose of the positive benefits of connected living.

Realizing how inadequate most of our homes are to accommodate future needs, it becomes crystal clear that it is critical for the O50s to take an inventory assessment by asking themselves what their priorities are for their future living spaces. How they will go about meeting these needs and wants? In other words, it is of the upmost importance to live life intentionally, by planned choices. Living life hoping that things will work out is not only foolishness; it is actually selfish when considering how the not planning will affect others!

This is the basic philosophy of Lifesizing which undergirds DESIGN SMARTS; living with a Mindset and an Attitude to prepare for a future equipped with the required tools for successful life transitions. And one of the most important tools in this toolbox of SMARTS is the enlightened MINDSET to vigorously, not haphazardly, seek the necessary preparations for what is next in their lives. For the majority of people, a coveted joyful and vibrant next life stage will not occur by the luck of the draw. Wisdom teaches us that, like all things in life, our situations are the direct result of whatever we have been sowing. Therefore, continually learning and implementing essential life tools will reap great rewards. These pioneering O50s will be the showpiece of DESIGN SMARTS living by enjoying an awesomely vibrant, rewarding, and fun life. In order to experience this coveted lifestyle, these SMART ones will be demanding homes that are:

- Functional
- Safer
- Flexible
- Intelligent
- Designed Smart
- Creative
- Energy Efficient
- Designed Green
- Designed to Recycle

The O50s will no longer accept present living models as they age because they are "pushing the envelope" rebels being a change making force to be reckoned with and taken seriously. Therefore, one of the numerous features of lifetime homes for married couples, or those living with a partner, will include dual master suites due to health issues or simply for better sleep. The Cadillac of these suites will also include separate water closets, dressing areas, and a shared sitting area. As this demographic wakes up to what is missing in their homes to promote a healthier, higher quality of living, many models of the past will go either unsold or undergo major upgrades to woo this newly enlightened homeowner.

Support lacking for single women in America

Then what about all of the single women? What types of housing options will they have? If there are no family arrangements for them and finances are tight, what can they do? Well, fortunately, there are many options available right now, and definitely more options developing, because this is an enormous population segment urgently needing better housing options.

Statistically, of the huge number of unmarried O50s, a disproportionate number are women. Sara Fix, who works for the AARP Public Policy Institute says, "That is what scares me, because I am one of those people and I do think about it." Kathleen Kelly, who runs the Family Caregiver Alliance in San Francisco, says she is seeing the same sort of concern in her social circle. "I'm in my 50s and my friends are all talking about, 'Could we all move in together? Could we buy an apartment building and all live together?' There are all sorts of permutations of this conversation," Kelly says. But it is really something people are thinking about, particularly women.

Leave it to this enterprising demographic of single O50 women to be part of a radical housing revolution. No longer is this age group living within the confines of former generations, as they age. They are putting their visionary minds to work and are forming housing options, like group houses. There is actually a *Boomer Housemates* entity along with GOLDEN GIRLS HOUSE movement. Lifestyle writer, Sharon Greenthal says, "Widowed, divorced, never married, childless, -there are many reasons why boomers in their 50's and 60's and beyond will find themselves living on their own as they age." In her online column she reports that "It is no wonder many older women choose to find roommates to share living expenses". This movement now has an online resource called Roomates4Boomers.com.

A major, exciting development of the housing revolution, to me personally, is Cohousing. According to the Cohousing Association of the United States (www.cohousing.org): "It is an intentional community of private homes clustered around shared space. Each family home has traditional amenities, including a private kitchen. Shared spaces typically feature a common house. Households have independent incomes and private lives, but neighbors collaboratively plan and manage community activities and shared space." One of the biggest benefits I love is that cohousing makes it easy to form clubs, organize child and elder care and carpool. There are tons more information on their very informative website.

Another aspect of the housing revolution is the wider acceptance, and in many cases the demand, for the "Connected Home" or smart home technology. As I read or hear about innovative advances for in-home technology that often make me shake my head in disbelief and amazement, they are a actuality a reality today! Examples of home technology that seem too far out there are systems that track personal medical information from one's toilet directly to a medical resource designed specifically for that patient. Yes, this is true, and this is not new news. It has been available for a few years and with the aging of America, it is only obvious that this will definitely be a smart home feature more readily available in the future.

Smart homes typically integrate all residential electronic systems throughout the home allowing for centralized control over entertainment, lighting, security, HVAC, window treatments, sprinkling systems, video cameras, plus communication with household members. The following is not new news to many but perhaps will be new news to chew on; the kitchen with a voice assistant! "Alexa, turn on cooking." When incorporated into a smart home system is capable of setting timers, bringing up kitchen lights, and much more. Connected appliances include things like the smart refrigerator with a camera that actually allows you to look inside your refrigerator, no kidding! If you're at the grocery store debating what is needed, just use your phone to check the refrigerator contents. Touch screens in the kitchen will be a common entity as predicted by the experts. The A Control14 Touch Screen will be integrated with the Intercom Anywhere application in the kitchen. It works as a video chat device, an intercom system, and a smart doorbell station.

To become aware of the unexpected, revolutionary, and delightfully different home-style models that are popping up across America is to live with DESIGN SMARTS.

Any discussion on the upcoming housing changes of today would be inadequately covered without acknowledging the several billion dollars spent yearly in the pet industry. It is no surprise that developers, such as Standard Pacific Homes, are offering pet suites. Their pet suite can be 170 square feet with a step-in wash station, handheld sprayer, tile walls and floors. It includes a designated drying area with a commercial size pet dry, a watering and feeding station, a large bunk-style bed plus a door that opens to a puppy run and of course, a flat screen TV. Now this may not be for the masses but, make no mistake about it, accommodating pets for the O50s is a huge priority that will only increase in design options. This is definitely an example of "follow the money" where the demand creates the supply.

Exciting housing models reflect the housing revolution happening In America

- Loft living
- Tiny homes
- Multi-gen homes
- Luxury apartments
- New condominium designs
- Shared housing
- Smaller homes
- Separate casitas
- Upgraded villas or patio homes

Sleek, modern apartments opened in Wichita's historic "College Hill". A *Wichita Eagle* article from September 23, 2018 says this complex is another exciting example of the results of the housing revolution of today. This complex will house 51 apartments on 3 floors with a fancy French/Italian restaurant on the ground floor. The O50s love the concept of a walkable neighborhood to restaurants, grocery stores, and entertainment possibilities that this apartment complex provides. Other apartment developers are offering a few of these features; but to my knowledge, none are offering total type of package. What knocked my socks off was this package of amenities; roof top patios, gated parking, resort-style salt water pool, community clubhouse, out-door kitchens, fitness center, pet-wash station, and a car-care center.

Warning: Do not be influenced by distractions

As more and more housing models and options become available, the O50s basic priority list, nevertheless, must be strictly maintained.

The Housing Revolution Is Upon Us

Homeowners are notoriously swayed or distracted by the bells and whistles that can override common sense. I have witnessed homebuyer's remorse more times than I can count in my design career due to a lack of knowledge or a commitment to their specific needs.

In the conclusion of this chapter, is my designer's take on why homeowners are so frustrated with their choices of housing in today's market. And at the top of my list of frustrations is the question, "Why do we keep doing the same basic plans with these design flaws?"

The top of the list of poor space planning leading to constant home frustrations are:

- Pass through laundry rooms from garage to kitchens that are inadequately functional and poorly designed.
- Non-functional storage.
- Large homes with tiny kitchen eating area or hearth rooms.
- Poorly designed kitchen islands.
- Outdated bathrooms with an over-sized Jacuzzi tub and small shower.
- Elaborate and expensive moldings versus luxury finishes and appliances.
- Minimum lighting throughout the interior and exterior.
- Unused basements.
- Inadequate walk-in closets.

It's apparent that things are changing quickly with the American profile. But what does this possibly have to do with any of us? It has everything to do with every one of us to become knowledgeable so we can navigate the choppy waters of our futures. To become aware of the unexpected, revolutionary, and delightfully different home-style models that are popping up across America is to live with DESIGN SMARTS.

These dramatically fresh and extraordinary trends are happening due, in part, to the changing American demographics of all age groups, but particularly the O50s. These statistics are having an unprecedented and enormous effect on the coming housing revolution with these new housing models.

> "More rooms and bigger spaces do not necessarily give us what is needed in a home. Houses should be designed to nurture, not impress"
>
> —Sarah Susanka

Remember the commercial, "What's in your wallet"? In closing this chapter, I ask you, "What is in your future for your housing dreams and goals"? Now that you are aware of your housing options, remove any of your own limits caused by perhaps your over reasoning and list the features you would absolutely love to have in your lifetime home?

 **REFLECTIONS**

What type of housing model appeals to you from the models listed in this chapter? _____

_____

_____

Write about your dream home of the future. Be bold. _____

_____

_____

_____

_____

_____

_____

_____

_____

_____

_____

S.M.A.R.T.S.

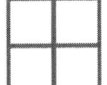 **SPACES.** Our spaces directly impact our lives. What is working in your home now? What is not?

 **MINDSETS.** Our lives directly follow our thinking. A positive mindset results in a positive life; a negative mindset results in a negative life. You get to choose.

 **ATTITUDES.** Our attitudes directly affect all and everything we do or become in our life. Age is just a number and you get to choose your attitude toward aging.

 **ROUTINES.** Our personal lifestyle in achieving wellness directly impacts our lives. Are you putting yourself first regarding your own personal life? You get to choose.

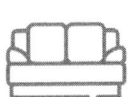 **TOGETHERNESS.** Our relationships directly affect our quality of life. Giving back to your community and others changes everything. You get to choose to live outside of your inner circle connections.

 **SPIRITUAL.** Our personal decisions about spirituality affects our outlook on life. Everyone believes in something—either your own power or a divine power.

MINDSETS

LIGHTING PLAN

CHAPTER 9

An Awakening

Downsizing your MINDSET to learn how to fight and to win your battle with those powerful fear giants named peace stealers and dream robbers!

My heart was pounding like a ticking time bomb ready to go off as I anxiously waited for the oncologist's diagnosis. "You have stage four metastasized melanoma," said the doctor. Wow! This was way worse than I had even anticipated hearing this gut-wrenching news on just how very serious the cancer was in my husband, Bob. My limited medical knowledge said stage 4 melanoma was a death warrant. Talk about our world changing drastically in a moment's time! We had so many questions with very few answers swirling in our heads as we nervously pondered our future. Admittedly, the first question was, is there even any hope to have for our future? Our minds were anxiously attempting to assimilate this scary "cancer" word let alone a stage 4 diagnosis. Then another bomb exploded in our ears with even more shocking news. We were told that there was no cure for melanoma, plus there was no predictable profile for melanoma meaning anything could happen at any given time since every case is completely unique. Where does this news leave Bob and Mitzi now?

It is necessary to explain that Bob had a skin melanoma removed in 1999 and lab tests of the margins around the removed skin melanoma were clear of cancer. Whew! However, and thankfully, his regular doctor recommended a lung x-ray every year since "melanoma likes to come back as lung cancer." For fourteen years, Bob had a lung x-ray and all were clear. In the fifteenth year, however, the radiologist said one lung spot appeared to be growing compared to the previous year's x-ray and recommended a needle biopsy.

The biopsy of the lung tumor confirmed melanoma. Bob was now taking morphine several times per day because of the pain caused by other tumors. Along with most people's fear, I was seeing firsthand the rigorous and ravaging effects of the cancer attacking his body. Was I in fear? You bet I was! It was time to let others know about the situation because we can't fight this by ourselves.

Grasping for a means to move forward, it was a survival necessity to evaluate all of these life altering questions starting with our emotional and mental MINDSETS. If there was any good to come of this horrible disease attacking Bob, it was our ability to discuss how we could tackle this explosive revelation about to take over our lives asking ourselves these tough questions. Is there any hope? What are the treatment options? How will we tell our family? How does this affect both of our lives professionally and personally? Are we going to collapse or buck up? Where will treatment be conducted? How much will insurance cover? How will this change our lifestyle? One of the toughest questions we asked each other was where do each of us want to live if one of us dies and we are alone?

How do we tell our adult kids that their father has very serious health issues? We couldn't tell one before the other, so we composed a lengthy email to all three and sent it. The phone rang within 2 minutes of sending the email with the first call. All were shocked and asked numerous questions like: where will you get treatment? Who is the best doctor? Is it terminal? Fortunately, we had a son living in The Woodlands, Texas.

An Awakening

Upon hearing of the situation, he immediately began the process of applying for treatment at the MD Anderson Cancer Center within the University of Texas Medical Center in Houston, Texas. People come from every country on earth to be treated at this hospital. Nevertheless, it was a known fact that people only go there when things are bad, very bad.

Bob's first appointment at MD Anderson was in early November. His assigned Doctor was a world-class melanoma expert with many, many research projects and years of treating patients with various types of melanoma. As Bob, our son and I sat in the exam room waiting on the Doctor; the tension was as expected, extremely heavy. Would MDA discover any other tumors that we didn't already know about? What was MDA's prognosis? We had to ask the question, "How long does he have to live?"

When the doctor walked in, she was noticeably unemotional as surely her field of medicine required. Her demeanor was very business-like and straight to the point. She didn't have many smiles. Obviously, this was serious. She basically confirmed what we already knew about the lung and rib tumors. Fortunately, nothing showed up in the brain.

We were stunned as we considered where to go from here. As treatment plans were further implemented, there were three significant questions that loomed in our minds. How were we possibly going to handle this emotionally and mentally (OUR MINDSETS)? How will Bob's physical health affect his professional life plus our personal life (OUR LIFESTYLE)? And how does this diagnosis affect where we will live now or in the future (HOMES AND LIVING SPACES)?

Fear Is Contagious

Of all of the questions we were struggling to answer, some of the hardest questions were how to deal with the reactions of our well-meaning family and friends. Did you know that you can hear fear? Giving grace to those understandingly concerned for us, we definitely heard the fear in their responses along with the expressions of doubt as Bob and I tried our best to keep a positive mindset moving ahead into our unknown future.

We would compare what was being said, and by whom, not for gossip sake or a judgmental response of what others were saying, but solely for us to reinforce in each other what we had established would be our course of action to fight this major fear from others that surrounded us. Please note that we understood others' fears as they were rightfully correct in the doom and gloom of Bob's diagnosis in their fears of losing Bob whom they loved. How were we going to answer all the myriad of questions coming our way was one of our biggest dilemmas?

Fear or faith

"Oh no, I just heard about Bob and want to know how you are doing Mitzi?" This was a very sensitive and difficult time for me trying to honor their concern without compromising my position of faith. Most of our well-meaning friends and family expected me to be in a panic or at the very least wrestling with the fear of what was going to happen with Bob. They were lovingly concerned for me and of course Bob but were focusing on how I was coping with what was considered a death sentence from Bob's diagnosis.

Admittedly, my initial response to Bob's report from his doctor was honestly, I am going to be a widow! My mind raced with how I would ever sell our home alone or even take care of all the financial details that Bob managed since this life-threatening event happened so suddenly.

Getting myself back to the steadfast grounding of my daily life, I did what I normally did even before cancer hit our lives, I prayed. This may seem like an obvious no brainer for a woman of faith; that is until one is paralyzed with the unknown but looming monsters that were attacking my mind trying to affect the way I dealt with Bob's deteriorating physical

An Awakening

condition. Seeing your husband unable to handle his pain, not eating or sleeping, barely able to communicate with me had me outside of my "normal". I gave myself grace to dive into the shock of Bob's reality.

Finally though, I realized that enough was enough. If I was going to be a tower of strength for Bob, it was going to take more strength than I could possibly ever possess on my own. In order to come along side Bob in this journey, there was no way unless I was standing strong, equipped in my faith? This sudden change caused a renewing of my mind with a determined mindset and attitude that the fear of my unknowns would not overcome my standing on faith for the strength to endure the months and even years of ahead.

Many criticized me for not dealing with reality when I answered the question "How are you doing Mitzi?" Often, I answered, "I believe for Bob's healing". This is shocking I know, unrealistic I know, perhaps even uncaring or selfish, I know. But my own personal reality on how I dealt with and am dealing with this new life is I am just fine, thank you. This is only because I made a covenant with myself to be strongly equipped with a new mindset and attitude of positive speaking and living throughout the unknown years ahead. But the most beautiful part of this equipping for our future is that Bob is right there with me. He is also incorporating a MINDSET of faith to carry us into our new mindset to live in faith versus living in fear.

The second of the three areas we needed to deal with was our lifestyle. What would be Bob's physical condition in his day to day status? Since even though he was well after the age of retirement for most people, Bob was still working full time. But now, would it be possible to continue his work schedule? At the onset of his treatments, he lost 20 pounds in a matter of 3 weeks validating the question of his work status. For most men, their careers are tied directly to their identity affecting their attitudes and self-worth.

If he was not going to be working, oh my, I was not ready to have a husband at home full time let alone dealing with his medical needs as well. This will sound terribly selfish and unloving I am sure to most of you. However, being transparently honest is my goal by not sugar coating my MINDSET and how our lifestyle could change. Being married for years involves each spouse establishing their own individual way of doing life when not together. Even if retirement is a planned event, there are major adjustments necessary in order for each spouse to navigate their new lifestyles. Listening to many other wives, I know that I am not alone with my MINDSET regarding how both our lifestyles could change and change drastically.

Along with our life altering decisions of the two areas above, what or where would our home be? At the time of writing this book, we lived a gloriously satisfying lifestyle in Cypress. In 2004 we bought an extremely run-down house built in the early 1930's in a lovely neighborhood. In renovating and restoring this older home over 2 ½ yeas, we spent time, effort, and money to achieve our goal of living in a home designed for not only aging in place, but also giving us a fabulous lifestyle.

As we answered the question of where each of us would want to live if one of us were alone, we both answered; not here in the perfect home for us as a married couple. No, we would need to reconfigure our next home. We would have to determine location, as well as what we both wanted and needed as we coped with replacing our truly beloved Cypress.

Answering these three questions is the essence of this book covering these main topics regarding wellness in our MINDSETS, our LIFESTYLES, and our HOMES. Wow! Whether or not we were ready to have these discussions, this unexpected major turn of events changed our entire world. We had to deal with all of these questions affecting how will we cope emotionally, our attitude toward this situation, Bob's physical status, how we will live with this disease, and how does this change where we will live? Will we have to move, downsize, etc.?

An Awakening

As I have written, we have made the decision to relocate to NE Ohio and to downsize not only in our SPACES but in our lifestyles. We are very excited about this move that will give us the freedom we want and need. Of course, we realize that there will be many challenges ahead in this new lifestyle with Bob's retirement to say the least. But we are determined to not let the dream robbers and peace killers keep us from moving forward with our plans.

Dream robbers not only try to side line personal goals, but they can rob you of achieving your professional dreams and goals.

I slayed the dream robber in my career

Preparing for our upcoming move got me thinking about some of the journeys I took to get here. One of the most important in my professional life was my decision to get my master's degree in interior design and get professionally certified—the key that would open many professional doors. It looked and felt daunting, but I pressed on. I adopted a new mindset that helped me fight the peace stealers, the dream stealers. They'll always be in your path. Sometimes you have to knock 'em down. I was determined—my mindset locked on getting that degree.

And oh, by the way, this was my dream when I was 46 years old with 3 kids at home, a booming interior design business, and a traveling husband. As much as the dream robbers wanted to use my life circumstances to distract me from achieving my goals, that's how determined I became to press on toward the prize.

After moving to Wichita, Kansas and after years of working for 3 different design businesses, I believed that in order to legitimize myself as a true professional, I needed to pursue a professional status through becoming A.S.I.D. (American Society of Interior Designers) certified.

I soon discovered that even though at that time—the early 1990's, living in Wichita, Kansas, with one university and two smaller colleges, there were no classes to help me accomplish my dreams and goals. As I continued to pursue my quest (since would you believe I had a BS in Home economics education), I was offered numerous times a teaching position. This is was flattering but frustrating as you can imagine.

Next, I courageously contacted ASID and after many, many phone calls plus a ton of hours seeking contacts, I finally had my application to apply for an ASID Allied standing which in itself is no small accomplishment. Why? Because it required a higher education degree, a minimum of 2 years of design experience, and 3 verified professional references. Holy cow already!

But the coolest part of all of this was receiving my first official ASID monthly magazine when low and behold there it was. Information on their national convention in San Francisco where a day long class was offered to study for the national qualifying exam (NCIDQ) to become my coveted goal to be professional interior designer. I could just see it on my business cards, Mitzi Beach A.S.I.D. So off I went to San Francisco.

Trying to look ever so sophisticated, I wore my very chic and stylish taupe wool long coat remembering that San Franciscans wore only black and basics, never bright colors. I had already made that embarrassing tourist mistake traveling to San Francisco being recently married, packing only whites and bright pastels. After all, it was summer in California, right? Not only was I freezing due to the bone chilling cold. I stuck out like a sore thumb. I had tourist written all over me.

Therefore, not to come close to another humiliating experience, I dressed the part and did a terrific job of fitting in or so I naively surmised. Then the architect instructor started giving instructions to the over-50 students in this class where again, I sat wide eyed and intimidated. And mind you, the class hadn't even started yet!

I thought for sure they were way better than me because no one smiled or did chit chat perhaps they thought it lowered their professional dignity.

An Awakening

Another sure sign was everyone had these very large portfolio bags, mostly in expensive looking leather that held architectural rulers, vellum, drafting triangles & pencils and etc. Like a kindergartener going to school, I had received my list of supplies proudly contained in my Office Max bag. With having no professional mentor or advising, I showed again how woefully incompetent I truly I was if I couldn't even do supplies with any class!

Since the instructor assumed we all had basic knowledge of drafting, programming, building codes, and space planning, he began from that level. I remember to this day how humiliated I felt believing that surely everyone was looking at me woefully fumbling through the assigned design project.

I lasted all morning but left midway in to the afternoon session demoralized, discouraged, and definitely feeling and believing that no one could be more stupid than I was to dream this goal.

For those of you that read my initial post on pursuing my goal of becoming a professional member of A.S.I.D (American Society of Interior Designers), you may remember this was my ending sentence from that post. For those of you interested in catching up to my long journey you can read the post here:

Fast forward a couple of years after my San Francisco debacle where my deflated designer self was believing that my dream was at a dead end since no one in Wichita was sharing my dream for obtaining professional status. Oh, there were a few professional ASID designers here, but they had no leads for me. Nevertheless, I kept hoping and believing that someday, something or someone would come along to help me.

In the 80's and 90's I used to go to Dallas Market twice a year for interior design sourcing with other Wichita designers. Unlike today 's home industry markets that provide tons of networking opportunities, it wasn't like that for me in those market days. I basically only did my design sourcing for my design business. The Brunschwig and Fil Dallas showroom was my favorite with stunning displays. One display was a sofa in their iconic fabric so frequently used by the very famous New York decorator, Sister Parish, that they named the fabric after her.

The B&F Dallas showroom was packed as usual, but I couldn't help but to hear an intense conversation between designers discussing the Q or the exam to qualify for professional ASID status. Of course, my radar was on full alert since they were talking my dream! However, this definitely was not a warm fuzzy conversation as this is what I heard: "I tried to do this exam, but it was so hard and time consuming that I literally took my hundreds of books and threw them in the trash!" Or: "I was so overwhelmed trying to study and do my design business that I gave up and put all those books in my closet never to see again, ever!"

Yes, I know without a doubt that I had that deer in headlight look. Nevertheless, I meekly approached this very disgruntled group of designers that I had never met, asking them how they knew who or where to go for preparing to take this Q exam? Suddenly, I had my hope back again getting from them a contact, Dr. Cheryl Meyer, professor at University of Central Ok. I had no idea of what I was about to encounter in this difficult, time consuming, expensive, and often discouraging journey of pursuing my dream of becoming a certified professional interior designer.

I connected with Dr. Meyer, she explained her $1200.00 fee for the exam preparation. Whew! I couldn't swing that amount then with 3 kids in college even with my booming design business. Bob and I had at that time over $50,000 yearly college costs and that was in the 90's so imagine what that would be in today's economy? But I was like a dog on bone contacting every lead I could in our area begging them to prepare to take the exam and share the costs bringing Dr. Meyer to Wichita, and we did.

Now, you might think this is the end of my story, but oh no, there's more of my saga. You see, Dr. Meyer was preparing me, but I had yet taken this rigorous exam. At that timing, there were 6 sections of this exam, given twice yearly at a designated place, proctored by a design

An Awakening

professional. Our assigned area was in Kansas City at Johnson Junior College, which is 3 hours from Wichita. Given that this exam is over 2 days, hotel and food expenses were in addition to the exam fee and books and etc. But onward and upward!

Finally, I was sitting for the infamous "Q" exam, short for the NCIDQ exam. Low and behold I passed 3 out of the 6 sections. Now, I had to wait 6 months to try again taking the remaining 3 sections. I studied at our kitchen table in our former family home "in my free time" of doing life, family, and did I mention my business was booming then?

Now this is my second try at this ultimate dream of mine when at the next exam opportunity, I passed 2 out of my 3 remaining sections yet to pass. Oh boy, could I possibly keep up my stamina and my enthusiasm to try for the third time to pass that last dreaded 3 D section? Yes, I did take this exam for the third time and I failed 3D by one stinking point! Seriously??

To say I was discouraged was the understatement, but now I had my fire back and I was mad as a hornet! There were no explanations, no guidance, no whatever's, when I traveled to University to Florida, yes, Florida, to seek a review and supposedly learn what I was doing wrong. To this day I remember being with the arrogant architect supposedly reviewing my 3D project. He looked at me and said, "I don't know what you expect me to do? I can't help you." I felt like I was right back where I started in San Francisco leaving Florida demoralized and discouraged. But there was one other emotion that kept me going and that was tenacity to not be this close and not have my dream regardless of the hurdles I had overcome and more ahead of me.

Well, the rest of the story is that I finally did indeed pass that rugged 3D section. Oh BTW, during this time, my designer friend, Liz Fleming and I traveled one day per week for a year and half to Edmond, Ok. also pursuing a master's degree in interior design as we both studied for the

ASID exam. And yes, we both graduated with our master's degree and yes, we both achieved professional status in ASID.

Can I hear an Amen?

Obviously, there is more to my story, but enough is enough already! Thank you for following along to my journey saga but my utmost purpose for writing this unusually long post is to emphasize that dreams are merely dreams if first and foremost, there is not an unwavering commitment to achieve that dream.

This could be your year to forge ahead accomplishing what is in your plan to achieve your dreams. Perhaps the saddest of all emotions would be to live with lifelong regret with the words "if only I had tried "tumbling around in my mind. Do not let this be you.

This quote from Teddy Roosevelt, the ALMANAC, has affirmed me many times to not listen to those dream killers whether from people or my own fear giants. My first book might not have lived up to my or anyone else's standard but to get back in the arena and try again with "my face marred by the dust… who errs … but if he fails at least he is daring greatly….

Live with no regrets all you dear O50s and at the end of it all, you can say that you tried, you did your very best, and you dared greatly. This is the sum total of achieving Design Smarts. Consider this quote from a speech given by Theodore Roosevelt, April 23, 1910.

> *"It is not the critic who counts; not the man who points out how the strong man stumbles, or where the doer of deeds could have done them better. The credit belongs to the man who is actually in the arena, whose face is marred by dust and sweat and blood; who strives valiantly; who errs, who comes short again and again, because there is no effort without error and shortcoming; but who does actually strive to do the deeds; who knows great enthusiasms, the great devotions; who spends himself in a worthy cause; who at the best knows*

An Awakening

in the end the triumph of high achievement, and who at the worst, if he fails, at least fails while daring greatly, so that his place shall never be with those cold and timid souls who neither know victory nor defeat."

CHAPTER 10

Above All, Get Wisdom

Until I started writing how downsizing applies to all the principles of DESIGN SMARTS, it hadn't occurred to me to connect the MINDSET principle to *downsizing* having less or fewer toxic thoughts. This was a "duh, Mitzi" revelation! My huge aha moment came as realized it was not enough for me to stop negative thinking but to downsize or eliminate them as they were exponentially multiplying in my O50 brain specifically attached to editing this book. This was a revelation to me. I needed to downsize my thoughts because with different times or different circumstances different thoughts enter our MINDSETS. I had already learned how our negative thoughts can potentially sabotage everything in our lives including our wellness, our relationships, our careers, and definitely our futures.

Now I know much more that I would like to share for your benefit as you enter new stages of life as an O50. Each stage of life comes with the obvious challenges since we have never experienced the positives and the negatives as we move through each life stage. There will be tons of new and different circumstances and the mind can work overtime if it is not downsized. Let me give you a very recent personal example.

It was a very cold morning and at 5:30 AM, prior to even getting out of bed to turn the heat up, before I put my feet on the floor, these thoughts came bombarding into my mind. *I'm not going to make my writ-*

ing deadline! There is too much to do and not enough time to do it. I know I am going to mess up this one and my only opportunity for signing books at the upcoming conferences. I am not possibly gifted enough to think that I could write a book. I am going to disappoint so many people who are counting on me to finish.

Mind you, even after all that I have learned, and put into practice, about mindsets, brain theory, and the power of our thoughts, these negative MINDSETS were my exact thoughts. How very easy it was for me to mentally crash into doubt, negativity, angst, discouragement, anxiety, and even fear. I allowed, or permitted, my deadline time pressures, coupled with the overwhelming fatigue from traveling the previous day, to control my mindset. These out of control thoughts distorted my thinking to a MINDSET that my day ahead would be one of doom and gloom. I felt a crushing fatigue and, along with a sour facial expression, my words made it worse. I told Bob how impossible my day was going to be, how little sleep I had, and on and on went my litany of self-pity. Can you relate?

The key is to master how to reset our MINDSETS to stop, think, then to respond. It's not life's circumstances that control our wellbeing in the midst of turmoil, it's our response.

Suddenly, only minutes later, after my doom and gloom hissy fit episode, it happened! I had been waiting on an email regarding the book cover image for this very book. In what to me was like a Nano second, I was smiling like a Cheshire cat and brimming over with delighted excitement as I viewed with absolute total glee the long-awaited image of my book cover. This almost tangible shift in my MINDSET changed my entire outlook on the day ahead. Just like that, I was transposed into a renewed MINDSET of one positive thought after another, each building upon the previous one, enabling me to see clearly where moments before, my mind was in a sullen, darkness of despair. I was spellbound in disbelief that this was my living room on my book cover and this book was really going to happen after all. Just like that, my physical countenance was full of joy as I described to my friends everything that I loved about the cover that my brilliant graphic designer had created. The life changing power to recognize that our thoughts control our entire being cannot be underestimated not only for all you O50s, but for everyone!

Equipped, Enlightened, Empowered

This chapter is intentionally under the section titled, Lighting Plan, to metaphorically connect our thinking or mindsets to lighting. In darkness, it is easy to stumble around losing our way, even bumping into unknown obstacles. With darkness often comes fear, whether real or imagined. In darkness, it is so easy to get confused by not being able to see at all. This metaphor is obviously indicative of how an unenlightened mindset operates when reacting to the never-ending circumstances of day-to-day life.

It's an amazing phenomenon that minds can either turn to a positive or a negative direction as quickly as turning on and off light switches. But herein lays the secret weapon to fight those traps, or button-pushing moments, making us succumb to these unwanted highs and lows. We can overcome this up and down, unstable MINDSET by becoming equipped with the empowering technique to immediately stop, and not react to life circumstances. Life happens all the time, the good, the bad and the ugly. But we can learn not to succumb as we experience new and different issues and life stages or circumstances like the one I shared in the opening paragraph. The key is to master how to reset our MINDSETS to stop, think, then to respond. It's not life's circumstances that control our well-being in the midst of turmoil, it's our response.

We get to choose, but it must happen instantly. Within minutes, we can be going down a slippery slope of self- pity or anxiety or doubt and despair. It is our choice to be pitiful or powerful, but we cannot be both at the same time. Charles R. Swindoll said, "Words can never adequately convey the impact of our attitude toward life. The longer I live, the more convinced I become that life is 10 per cent what happens to us and 90 per cent how we respond to it." Can I hear an amen?

Does your mindset have a dimmer switch?

Dimmer switches on lighting fixtures control the level, or the amount, of light needed for various activities whether soft, ambient lighting for relaxing or brighter lighting for working or cooking. Likewise, some people have no dimmer switches when it comes to how they react to anything, or anyone, in life. These are the people in your life that routinely react to life circumstances with an explosive comment, body language, moodiness, withdrawal, or name-calling. It really doesn't matter if the car doesn't start or the doctor's report is very serious, their reaction is the same, uncontrollable intensity.

Loose cannons seem to be everywhere today with road rage, as an example, at an all-time high, often with disastrous consequences. These are the folks without a dimmer switch for their MINDSETS. Their minds are consistently on full wattage making being around them like maneuvering a minefield waiting for the bomb to explode. What comes out of their mouths, or their behavior, is the first thought in their minds. Nothing in life happens without first thinking, then speaking or acting, what is thought about first. Therein lays the indisputable fact that out of the heart, the mind speaks. Our words are our verbal thoughts heard.

> "Don't hang out with angry people; don't keep company with hotheads, Bad temper is contagious—don't get infected."
>
> —Proverbs 22:24

Some of us grew up in families, full of angry people, without a verbal regulating dimmer switch. To undo any pattern of modeled or learned behavior takes tons of effort, with the key being the recognition of any of those residual negative behaviors. The very worst toxic mindset is to believe the lie that no change is possible. This is simply not true!

A lot of us creative people are highly emotional beings with very strong feelings. Through my faith and my mentors, my mind is renewed daily; as new patterns of thinking, feeling, and speaking guide my world. I am not, in any way, saying that I always get it right on responding versus reacting. But I am saying that I am finally making huge progress with this life changing principle. I am sure my family and close friends are thinking, it's about time.

Controlling my mind, by first taking a pause before I even utter a word, is helping me with my relationships of course; but the biggest reward is my own beautiful peace and contentment. Therefore, this is why there's an entire chapter devoted to MINDSETS. In order to live a life with DESIGN SMARTS, developing control over mindset is the basis for any real change to occur; regardless if it is to happen in the home or in any of life's various venues. Without a doubt, controlling our thoughts is the beginning of wisdom for absolutely everything we will ever do or be in life.

Mindsets control the blueprint of life

No self-respecting builder, architect, or interior designer would begin a new project without a blueprint. However, do you acknowledge that the power of your thoughts is the actual controlling blueprint for your life?

"As the mind goes, life follows" is not just a saying to be tossed about lightly. For instance, do you say that you are going to do such and such; but in reality, not even you believe this "whatever" will actually be your own reality? I have learned the hard way that I must absolutely believe, with all my heart and mind that I will indeed accomplish what I say that I should accomplish. In other words, no pun intended, I can fool others with my words; but in no way can I fool either my unbelief or my belief in what I say, without first mentally believing it myself.

Regret leaves a very bitter aftertaste as a result of failing to accomplish a dream, goal, or lifestyle. But in reality, was there really a steadfast mental commitment and belief that, against all odds, those pounds would be shed, that organizing would be done, or that relationships would be restored? This is the power that your mental blueprints possess, like a rudder on a ship, navigating the direction of your life in absolutely every single area and absolutely every single stage of your life. But how much attention do you give to what you are thinking, watching on TV, reading, being influenced by social media, or what others are saying? You get to choose what you are thinking about and what thoughts you allow to marinate in your mind.

The best news ever

The best news that I have been blessed beyond measure to learn is about all the current advances in brain theory research. One of the respectable leaders in this exciting field of brain research is Dr. Caroline Leaf. In her books and video series she describes the revolutionary knowledge that the brain does not have to decline as we age after all. But here is the challenge; almost everyone believes this misconception that as we age, our memory is compromised. We have all heard the use it or lose it phrase, which is exactly how our brains can continue to grow dendrites (roots or brain connective tissue that helps determine behavior and memory) as we learn new information or form new habits. And the opposite is also true; the brain loses existing dendrites without continual thinking and analyzing life on a continual basis. Sitting in front of the TV, in a passive state, or watching YouTube, or being isolated without personal interaction does not help the brain to age well.

Isn't this exciting news? O50s can certainly achieve so much more than those outdated and unsubstantiated beliefs that previously convinced us that memory loss is just a fact of life. This good news allows each of us to choose what happens to our memory by learning these new factual developments regarding our brain potential at any age. Read or listen to Dr. Leaf's scientific research and studies over decades, of her medical practice and learn for yourself how awesome this good news is, especially for the O50s with so much life ahead. This powerful knowledge can reset your mind as you take hold of this bold new perspective on what is truth, versus assumptions, on the brains capacity to do much, much more throughout all of life.

The clock is ticking for all of us and it is critical timing to change or get a new MINDSET on aging and preparing for the future. This is such a hard message to deliver. But again, I believe that those who are aiming to age powerfully will not only receive this message but will also adopt a new MINDSET for themselves. Not one single person in this whole universe can do this for anyone but himself or herself. Only the individual can control his own MIND; and where his MIND goes, his future will certainly follow.

You can live your wisdom

It is no secret that most interior designers are right-brain thinkers, which means having a creative mind versus a logical, technical, math-kind of mind. And for sure, that describes me, a right-brain, creative visionary! But why would this be part of a chapter on MINDSETS? Well years ago,

I began observing, in my interior design business, that my clients' homes were, for the most part, not meeting their needs on so many levels. I would get very frustrated at the wrongness of what is offered in home spaces today and even more frustrated when the client wanted me to "just make it all better" for them. How does one make a huge wrong a right? I started processing how, easily, over three-fourths of what I see in the homes of family, friends, and clients is grossly inadequate to meet their needs. And this was even before my passion developed for wanting to prepare others for setting up their homes for their later years.

"Bingo!" I'll do a blog, and write, and photograph on these exact issues. I'll get out there and teach and educate and inspire others to think about their homes in ways not previously considered. I then thought, *You have not the slightest idea how to do all the technical requirements to have an online blog.*

What are URLs, domains, and so on?" Thus, began this huge battle with my MINDSET. How in the world would I learn, and be able to do, the myriad of technical skills required? I knew already that it takes me ten times longer than most people to learn and relearn in order for any concept to actually stick in my right-brain mind. I would get so utterly discouraged and overwhelmed and it would have been so easy to just pitch this whole idea and say, "Nice try, but this is just way too hard, and why are you possibly thinking you can pull this off, anyway? Who do you think you are at 'your age,' doing what all those younger and much smarter techie bloggers are already accomplishing...really, Mitzi...get real with yourself!"

"For as he [or she!] thinks in his heart, so is he."

—Proverbs 23:7

Exactly!

Day in and day out, my MINDSET had to keep believing that I can do and learn whatever I needed to accomplish my passion and goal of helping others do it differently and do it better on aging in America. How did I do this? Well, first off, I am a strict believer in knowing that whatever I do not know, there are others who certainly do. The challenge, of course, was finding those that could help me. But, eventually, they came into my life. Bob has definitely pitied them as they scratched their heads or rolled their eyes at my total incompetence!

It soon became very obvious that I had to simply make up my mind to do what I believed I was called to do. Regardless of how tedious and frustrating this endeavor was, my passion to help others would be worth it! I must keep on trying, messing up, trying again, messing up—and still to this day, that is my pattern since I mess up a lot!

Where our mind goes, our life will certainly follow

If we allow negative thoughts to dominate our mindsets, such as: "I am too old, I am too far gone in my health to have a chance again, I don't have the money, I don't have the skills or education," we certainly will stay stuck exactly where we are. This is so sad, and so unnecessary and futile, when a new mindset can open up a new life potential that we never dreamed possible.

We were created to be visual beings. This means if we can see something in our minds, visualize it, we can move toward that image. Therefore, if we see ourselves as unhealthy or fat, stuck in a mundane life, plodding through our days, guess what? That mental vision is exactly what will be the reality until, and unless, a new MINDSET or a new vision is formed. Until we can see it, I believe it simply will not happen.

I see myself going higher and higher in my technical skills. I see myself getting healthier and healthier, not weaker and plagued with aging symptoms. I see my children and grandchildren successful. Argue all you want, but this works. I am the example of this premise of visualization and belief that I can and I will accomplish my goals. Time will tell on my own personal story, and you will witness whether I make it or not, but regardless, I am all in!

My MINDSET, however, tells me that what I am visualizing for my future will indeed surely follow. And I am certainly no smarter, richer, better educated, or more connected than anyone else. I am simply one O50 lady that has made up her MIND to age differently and to age better in America. AND, to bring along with me all those of you who have also MADE UP THEIR MINDS to age differently and age better in America. I can see (visualize) it all now. Can you?

Even though I pay extra for supplemental insurance, a doctor refused to see me simply because I was insured by Medicare. No matter, I am now a Medicare person as far as the health care industry is concerned. While this affects many other O50s too, I needed to assess my new health status and, most definitely, change my own personal MINDSET regarding how I approach getting older. I do not hear many of my fellow O50s talking about this bigger-than-life issue of aging and medical denial. Are they all going to be as shocked, and even stunned, as I was when they hear "Sorry, we are not taking any more Medicare patients"?

Right then and there, I made the choice to change my MINDSET on how I proceeded towards my future. No more just assuming that all is well, and all will work out in regard to my health care options. I am a very positive person and a woman of deep and ever-growing faith who believes I will indeed have a beautiful future ahead, regardless of my age. But I also see reality when it smacks me right in the face! "Sorry, we are not taking any more Medicare patients."

Live your wisdom by knowing DESIGN SMARTS

What do George W. Bush, Bill Clinton, Laura Bush, Loni Anderson, Dolly Parton, Liza Minnelli, Jimmy Buffett, Donald Trump, Diane Keaton, Tommy Lee Jones, and me, yours truly, have in common? We are all part of the elite group—the oldest of baby boomers. Now you might ask, "So what does this have to do with DESIGN SMARTS?"

Well, take a look at these and others in this elite group of the leading edge of this O50 generation and see for yourself who has had the mindset of aging with DESIGN SMARTS. Now, of course, life happens. We all acknowledge that, regardless of lifestyle, physical issues do indeed occur. But, in general, we are what we have lived in mind, body, and spirit. There is just far too much evidence to prove the following strong statement declaring we have a say in our futures by our MINDSETS!

> "You can do anything you decide to do. You can act to change and control your life; and the procedure, the process is its own reward."
>
> ~Amelia Earhart

Remember: Where our mind goes, our life will certainly follow.

The Mayo Clinic online newsletter published an interesting chart that highlights the power of positive thinking.

NEGATIVE THOUGHT	POSITIVE THOUGHT
I've never done it before.	It's an opportunity to learn something new.
It's too complicated.	I'll tackle it from a different angle.
I don't have the resources.	Necessity is the mother of invention.
It's too radical to change.	Let's take a chance.
I'm not going to get any better at this.	I'll give it another try.

The good news is this wonderfully empowering fact: it is never too late to change our MINDSETS about aging and begin again. We are so amazingly resilient in mind, body, and spirit that anything is possible if we change our minds regarding how we will age. Researchers continue to explore the effects of positive thinking and optimism on health, and this is exactly what having a DESIGN SMARTS mindset is all about.

Also, according to the Mayo Clinic the health benefits of a healthy mindset include:

- Increased life span.
- Lower rates of depression.
- Greater resistance to the common cold.
- Lower levels of distress.
- Better psychological and physical wellbeing.
- Reduced risk of death from cardiovascular disease.
- Better coping skills during hardships and times of stress.

New research on brain theory reveals that our bodies respond in a physical way to our words. I know, really? Yes, really and I would encourage you to research on your own the new developing brain theories. Connecting the mind to body to speaking is emerging as an exciting new dimension in controlling our lives. Yes, to many it sounds ridiculous, like voodoo or the like. However, Dr. Caroline Leaf and many other esteemed medical researchers and scientists have convinced thousands of skeptics in their sound research and clinical practice using these exact theories. The results have been considered miraculous, as can be verified in Dr. Leaf's books. These two books, using sound study and research, proved to me that my words do indeed have power to change my life in untold ways. As more and more brain theory emerges, we are seeing in brain scans images of actual dark clusters representing toxic thoughts versus what a healthy brain shows. Do your own research and be prepared to be utterly amazed when you discover the power our thoughts and words have on our emotional, mental, and physical wellbeing. Therefore, I firmly believe the following:

Our mind is our mental house

Declaring and designing your best life all starts in the mind. Right now, right this minute, you can make up your mind to have a fabulous future. This is possible if we believe with a new MINDSET, we can be healthy as we age. Along with learning and embracing new lifestyles that daily restore our energy, we can raise our quality of life by the intentional and functional planning of our future.

By believing that, with a new MINDSET, we can live in homes that daily restore our energy and quality of life. Our mind is our mental house. Our life will follow our thoughts or MINDSETS. Therefore, to remodel or upgrade our mental houses is a very DESIGN SMARTS thing to do.

Knowledge is just knowing, without understanding, how or what to do with what we know. With the transferring of knowledge to understanding, wisdom happens. In a humorous kind of way, my late dad used to say about some intellectuals that they didn't have enough common sense to get in out of rain. In essence, he was saying unless knowledge is applied, their wisdom lacks the understanding to even get out of the rain. My dad grew up during the Depression. Like many kids he had to quit school after the eighth grade to earn money and work the family farm to put food on the table. But I do not know many people that were smarter than he was due to his uncanny ability to apply what he knew. My dad had the wisdom to apply his understanding to life that benefited all of us who took the time to listen to him.

Gaining knowledge yields wisdom. As we apply wisdom to life, we are living in understanding. In other words, we do what we know is necessary. Many intelligent people make some of the stupidest lifestyle choices. Education is facts and information. Wisdom gives principles, solutions, answers and special insight to know what to do. This understanding is what is necessary for the O50s to successfully maneuver their lives to reap the sweet, sweet benefits of applying their wisdom.

So, have you ever really thought about committing to your future successes with your thoughts and your words? I do this MINDSET for thinking and speaking all the time. The way I see it is, what do I have to lose? Would you consider declaring over your life these declarations? But remember, you have to believe it!

For your health

- I DECLARE that my health is getting stronger and better daily.
- I DECLARE to eat in order to live my very best life for myself and in order to be my best for those I care so much about.
- I DECLARE to daily live in peace and joy as you control the stresses of your life.
- I DECLARE I will exercise and are experiencing renewed energy and released stresses.

- I DECLARE a new lifestyle of getting eight hours of sleep and practicing a balanced life, to live my best life now and in my future.

For your home

- I DECLARE I will have a personal restorative sanctuary space in my home.
- I DECLARE that my present or future home will take me into my future years with style, dignity, and a fabulous quality of life.
- I DECLARE that my present, or future, home will give me so much joy that it renews and restores my energy daily.
- I DECLARE that my present, or future, home provides all my physical needs now and in the future.

"Do this: Above all and before all, get wisdom! Write this at the top of your list: Get understanding. Throw your arms around her – Believe me, you won't regret it, never let her go – She'll make your life glorious!"

—Proverbs 4:7

REFLECTIONS

1. If you could let yourself dream big for doing or becoming something, what would it be? _____

   _____

   _____

   _____

   _____

   _____

2. How long has your mind been entertaining the "what ifs" for this dream or goal? _____

   _____

   _____

   _____

   _____

3. What would it take for you to seriously consider your first steps in making your dream or goal a reality? _____

_____

_____

_____

_____

_____

4. If you could be truly honest with yourself, what really is holding you back from pursuing your dreams or goals? _____

_____

_____

_____

_____

_____

_____

_____

_____

_____

S.M.A.R.T.S.

 SPACES. Our spaces directly impact our lives. What is working in your home now? What is not?

 **MINDSETS.** Our lives directly follow our thinking. A positive mindset results in a positive life; a negative mindset results in a negative life. You get to choose.

 **ATTITUDES.** Our attitudes directly affect all and everything we do or become in our life. Age is just a number and you get to choose your attitude toward aging.

 **ROUTINES.** Our personal lifestyle in achieving wellness directly impacts our lives. Are you putting yourself first regarding your own personal life? You get to choose.

 **TOGETHERNESS.** Our relationships directly affect our quality of life. Giving back to your community and others changes everything. You get to choose to live outside of your inner circle connections.

 **SPIRITUAL.** Our personal decisions about spirituality affects our outlook on life. Everyone believes in something—either your own power or a divine power.

ATTITUDE

SELECTION PHASE

Chapter 11

A Cluttered Mind No More

Have you ever considered reducing or eliminating or *downsizing* those negative, stinking thinking attitudes regarding aging? I know this is very hard to do in our present environment of shortsighted attitudes or paradigms present in America today. My mission is to help you do just that very thing, to *downsize* any self-defeating attitudes you may unknowingly or knowingly say or think about your aging. What is rather humorous is that even in our forties, aging is happening as it is happening to every living soul no matter his or her age. What is not very humorous however, is that it is considered by many marketers or advertisers that to even mention or write about aging is the kiss of death.

However, in order to have your home and your lifestyle become the vehicles that power you through all your years ahead, downsizing your aging attitudes is an absolutely critical part to be rocking life regardless of your age.

This chapter will cover how the attitudes you have on your home and in your lifestyle will directly affect how you age. It is a great time to be in the O50s stage of life since there are so many wonderful new ideas, products, and designs to make your next years be your best years. Do not miss out! *Downsize* any of your *previous* misconceptions and outdated attitudes on aging to become part of this exciting new DESIGN SMARTS movement.

Attitudes in our homes

I was recently having a conversation with a couple of my older O50 clients who are in their early sixties. I asked if I could review their new house plans to see if there were areas to upgrade for their future years. Without a second's hesitation, their response to my design suggestions was, "Oh, we'll do those things later." And their response was in such a firm, non-compromising tone of voice that I knew this conversation was forever closed. Furthermore, I was not to bring this up again.

What does "we will do those things later" really mean? I think it actually means: Don't bug me, Mitzi. I am not going to fall in my bathroom. I'm also not going to have surgery or knee or hip replacement or an accident that prevents me from using my bathroom. Come on, I don't want to hear about this bathroom upgrading. And furthermore, I do not want to consider doing the changes or upgrades that you are encouraging me to do. Don't bug me with these upgrades for this future use stuff!

Attitudes about our health

When we were in our 60's, before Bob was receiving cancer treatment drugs, we were at dinner with friends our age and the conversation came up about what meds we were on, as if this is a normal dinner conversation. We said none, really, and they couldn't believe we were not at least on high blood pressure medicine or a statin to control our cholesterol or any arthritis meds. Their comment: "Well, every one of our friends is taking at least some of these, just like us" carried the underlying message: "Everyone else is like us, so what's the big deal here?" Now please understand I most assuredly accept the reality that many people definitely need their medications for all kinds of medical issues.

But what was really being expressed here? I think our friends' comment illustrates the American attitude for way too many, which is: You get older, you have an issue, and you go to the doctor and get meds for it. Period, end of story. Don't talk to me about changing my ways or my lifestyles. I am just like everyone else!

Again, please know that I do not want to offend anyone taking medications. This is a chapter on how attitudes affect all aspects of life so read on and don't throw this book at me!

In planning an extensive and very expensive kitchen remodel, I asked the client how they would use their kitchen, meaning how they worked their daily cooking. The answer was, "Oh, for delivery or take-in foods and maybe just cook lunch or breakfast here. We go out to eat almost every night." But what was really being said here, and what was the attitude? It was probably: Are you kidding me? Cook with our crazy schedule? Or: It's just me or just me and my spouse, so why would I go to all that trouble? Seriously, Mitzi, that is so not the way we are going to live at this stage of life."

Sadly, this is very common, no matter the economic level. As we all well know, the fast food service statistics and the frequency of eating out appears to be the main eating routine in the American daily diets. But this is not true for those with a DESIGN SMARTS ATTITUDE No way are they getting sucked into that self-defeating pattern of thinking.

A DESIGN SMARTS attitude sounds like:

In the home

While looking at a possible new home purchase with clients who wanted to evaluate the appropriateness of the home's layout for their stage of life, the wife said, "I know we will have to remodel this master bathroom. Look how narrow this door is and check out this way-outdated and unsafe shower. We may not do it right away, but we know we have to do this upgrade." This wise client grasped the concepts and realities of implementing safety features to lessen potential accidents. She also wisely recognized other design features that will benefit her every day for years to come. This client has a DESIGN SMARTS attitude.

In Health

A friend was telling me about how his doctor prescribed a statin drug for high cholesterol, a prescription he did not fill. He wanted to try diet and exercise first to see if the drug was necessary. After he changed his diet and eating routines, at the next checkup the doctor says, "Great job, your cholesterol is down from 200 to 185. The statins are working." My friend never filled that prescription but took the bull by the horns and said, "I am going to be proactive with my health and not start this long road of one med after another." This reflects DESIGN SMARTS attitude, for sure.

I was once doing a TV taping on Boomer Smart Cooking, showing how easy it was to prepare a simple, healthy, yummy, and fast meal. The comments I kept hearing were: "This is so easy if I could just plan my meals instead of waiting until I am exhausted at the end of my day. I am so tired, then I give in and stop and pick something up that I know is not good for me."

Therefore, at the very top of my suggestions to experience a fun filled, healthy, life long-term living is having a DESIGN SMARTS attitude. This is the key to ageless living. And I definitely believe this key to ageless living is for everyone regardless of whatever life stage, health or home status. Throughout these previous chapters, I have stated that there is always something that can be done to improve the quality of life. I will stand on this premise as long as I have voice to do so whether in speaking or writing. No matter what, with a smarter and higher-level attitude, life can indeed be improved.

Attitudes do affect aging

This is what I call the Triple A's of getting older; Attitudes, Affect, Aging. I have spoken on this for years, watching those in my class or audience, waiting for the light bulb to go on for the ones that get it. And inside, I am cheering a big "yes" for them! But have you ever watched someone silently but visibly, with their facial expressions or body language, tell you: "Lady, you are smoking bananas here and I am not buying one word of what you are telling me?" Well, I certainly have because what I believe, teach, and write says that aging is all about our own attitudes. Sorry to say, many adamantly do not want to hear this because it wipes out all their excuses.

I know this may sound harsh and that is not my intention at all. But sometimes it is necessary to take the bull by the horns and tell it like it is. Underneath every single word in this book is the sincere heartfelt goal to hopefully inspire and educate others to do and be more in their life stages. And yes, perhaps I should be ducking here, but I have always been out there in my thinking, believing, and doing. Why else, for heaven's sake, would I even be doing this whole aging thing in the first place? I do this because I care deeply about your future welfare and well-being. If this effort helps even some of you to open your eyes and ears to what is happening in America and motivates you to do what is needed to prepare for these changes, then it is all definitely worth it.

> "Don't try to be young. Just open up your mind. Stay interested in stuff. There are so many things I won't live long to find out about, but I'm still curious about them"
>
> ~Betty White in her 90's

If any change is ever going to happen, it must first begin in our minds. This is why we must examine our attitudes and not our circumstances. It is time for us to shake off that stinking thinking old age mentality. It is time for us to choose to rise above the stereotype of aging in America and become the new normal by aging with style, dignity, class, and, most importantly, influence. So how are you preparing for your future? Are you even thinking about your future let alone preparing for it? Well, if your answer is simply a "no", you are not alone. Unfortunately, that is my huge concern for my fellow O50s because in just a few short years, what we have come to expect of our government may not be the new reality regarding Social Security or Medicare, which has been historically relied upon by millions of Americans.

We all have the power within ourselves to change. Remember our O50 history that changed America when all the war babies were born? Remember Woodstock? And remember the beginning of rock and roll that made "the establishment" shudder? However, the adage that our strengths can also be our weakness is sadly true for this ambiguous O50 demographic. Many believe they will never age, and if they do, it will be on their terms. Nice philosophy, except unfortunately this is not reality, not even for the infallible O50s. Very few things in life just happen without our preparation to make things happen. Aging well is absolutely an example of this principle.

Change your attitude and change your life.

About ten years ago, I was at a gathering of some very accomplished and professional interior designers. Don't even ask me why, but I stuck my silly neck out to bring up social media skills as being very critical to our business futures. I was shocked and dismayed at the litany of excuses that circulated around the room.

"Well, you won't catch me putting my personal information on Facebook!"

"Well, I've heard that it's even personally dangerous!"

"Social media is so silly and childish; like who cares if I am having coffee at Starbucks?"

"Why would I ever do that now at my age?" (Meaning: "I am doing quite fine just the way I have always done my business, thank you very much.")

And there was the emphatic shaking of heads of those seated around the table as they agreed with these statements. This made me sad to realize how closed-minded many older adults' attitudes can be to change, to new ideas, or to learning new things. This un-teachable, closed mind attitude frequently stems from either being misinformed or from having a prideful arrogance which is really saying or thinking, "I am doing just fine so don't mess with me."

And it is amazingly sad to me that those conversations thwarted any discovery of the amazing potential and scope of other social media platforms in addition to Facebook—like blogs and professional connections on Instagram, LinkedIn or Twitter—to reach other professionals, trade and vendor opportunities. No, social media is definitely not all about "I am having coffee at Starbucks." Certainly, I am not promoting Facebook and social media for everyone. I am merely giving an example of what an inflexible attitude sounds like in every day conversations.

Garbage in, garbage out

Everyone has heard the phrase "garbage in/garbage out" in regard to what goes in our minds, computers, bodies, and so forth. In other words, what we allow into any of these areas is exactly what comes back out. What does any of this have to do with a DESIGN SMARTS Attitude? Well, if we listen without a discerning ear to what is being said around us, it is very, very easy to just go with the flow in agreement even if it is passive agreement of what everyone else is thinking or doing. It is also very, very easy to eat the garbage by agreeing to what others are saying just because they are our friends, family, associates, or even colleagues. To excel on an individual higher personal level, there must be security filters to evaluate both positive and negative words and thoughts that have the immense potential to direct life choices.

9 attitudes that keep us stuck in the mire of garbage thinking:

I'm getting old and I just can't change who I am or what I do, for heaven's sake!

- I don't have time to exercise. I'm too busy already.
- I don't have the time or money to work on anything in my house.
- This is the way I've always done things, and I don't need any help or anyone telling me how to live my life.
- My time is valuable, and I'd like to be with my family and friends and do what I want to do. Why would I consider helping a food bank or neighborhood school? Let all those do-gooders get out there and do their thing.
- All my friends look like I do.

- Starting a home remodeling project is just unrealistic. Where would the money come from, and why would I even consider changing the way things are now?
- Everyone I know around my age is on blood pressure medicine and a statin drug. You are crazy telling me I can get off these drugs with a change in my lifestyle.
- When I am older, I will think about what to do with my bathroom. I certainly do not need to be upgrading for safety now.
- Well, if I need financial help when I am older to make changes for my health or a place to live, my Medicare and Social Security benefits will take care of me.

Every one of these stinking-garbage-type patterns of thinking keeps our attitudes stuck; thereby thwarting the potential for many opportunities for enrichment and growth.

Those aging with DESIGN SMARTS attitudes however, are empowered, equipped, and are enlightened with wisdom and understanding and are asking:

- What does my future look like?
- What changes should I be making now to be healthier in the future?
- Where will I live? Can I stay in my current home conveniently and safely?
- Do I ever think about leaving a legacy of influence for others that lives to give?

This is one of the most critical components of someone with a DESIGN SMARTS attitudes. They know that they should not eat the mental conversational garbage swirling around them everywhere. And they know they don't have to agree with everyone in "their herd" just because they all think, look and speak alike, or act in agreement. The movers and the shakers in ageless aging are fighting hard to not give in and just look like all their friends who have just, you guessed it, given in to aging like everyone else. But apathy and indifference are contagious. Do not hang out with these people or you can easily have their garbage thrown at you in very insidious and unsuspecting ways. Don't hang out with those people who are stuck thinking, looking, speaking, or acting in ways that go against all the DESIGN SMARTS attitudes on ageless aging.

We all have one or two negative people are in our lives, like a boss or family member. But we do not have to seek them out over and above what is absolutely necessary. I have been in these situations too many times to count as a result of personal or business obligations. This, however, doesn't mean we give lip service to agreement or, heaven forbid, do what the slackers are doing just to go along with the herd. This is tough talk. But so is a diagnosis of Type 2 diabetes often due to being too many pounds overweight; or eating like everyone else or falling in a grossly inadequate bathroom requiring many surgeries and physical therapy. Who do you want to be around? Who do you want to be like? The really cool thing is we get to choose! No one can choose our attitudes. It is up to each of us whether we choose to further our life with O50 DESIGN SMARTS Attitudes.

> "Wise men and women are always learning, always listening for fresh insight."
>
> —Proverbs 18:15

We get to choose

Did you know that you can hear and discern others' level of maturity? Yes, it is true. What are these markers of speaking that reveal a person's level of maturity and wisdom? Their words…listen to their words.

> **Low-Level Thinkers** Talk about other people and themselves a lot.
> **Mid-Level Thinkers** Talk about events and themselves a lot.
> **High-Level Thinkers** Talk about theories and analysis of what is happening, and concepts and philosophies or beliefs.

All of us fall into all three categories at one time or another, but where we are speaking the majority of the time determines our level of maturity and wisdom. With this in mind, whom do we want to hang out with when we can have an option to choose? Well, for sure, those equipped with DESIGN SMARTS know to avoid those that are:

- Indifferent
- Negative
- Complacent
- Grouchy
- Un-teachable
- Uncaring
- Stagnant

O50s with DESIGN SMARTS seek out other who are:

- Motivated
- Positive
- Compassionate
- Pleasant
- Teachable
- Caring
- Growing

Did you ever think about what you are thinking about? Did you know that you can actually choose what to think about? Most definitely, our thoughts can be controlled. For example, someone pulls out in front of me while I am driving. I can actually choose my ATTITUDE or my thinking on how I will react. Will I shake it off and be grateful that I am not hurt, or will I become very angry, thinking all sorts of non-printable adjectives toward that driver? It most certainly is my choice to choose how I will think in that very split second.

Recently, Bob had a very restless night, getting up many times and waking me up. After about 4:30 AM, I knew getting back to sleep was not happening. I got up at 5:30, which is not uncommon when I have had a good night's sleep; but getting up at 5:30 on a poor night's sleep can set me up to think not-so-good thoughts mostly aimed right at Bob. But I have learned the power of choice in my thoughts. Determined to not let my lack of sleep ruin my day (or Bob's), I did a lot of self-talk. "This will be a great day, Mitzi. You will get your writing done today as planned. You can take a twenty-minute nap later." The opposite is also true if I complain all day being tired and grouchy rationalizing to others that I am just so tired, then I will be tired and me, myself and I will be grouchy all day.

I have found controlling my thoughts to be one of my life's biggest challenges because my thoughts become my words and my words become my behaviors. Watch what words you are saying and see if this isn't the reality of how you act. Choosing what I choose to think about is critical to my well-being, my health, my relationships, my business, and all of my entire life. My thoughts determine my ATTITUDE on every single thing in my life now and in my life for the future.

Again, and again research, such as the huge Women's Health Initiative at the Pittsburgh School of Medicine involving over 100,000 women, tells us that a positive attitude affects our health. Those with a positive attitude were less likely to have heart disease because there is a definite mind-body connection. Just tell yourself in your self-talk, or your thoughts, that you don't feel well and watch how your day turns out. Now of course we all have days where we are not up to par or are fighting the common cold.

But I am a firm believer that how I respond to what my physical state is reflecting will, without a doubt for me, determine whether I go down for the count or simply give myself permission to have a "restore Mitzi" day. That's a totally different mindset and ATTITUDE!

This, for me, is one tough daily battle. Every day is a new day with a new set of situations to be "thought about." Some days I win my mental-thinking battles and some days I lose big time. I hate those days when I give in to self-pity, discouragement, frustration, and insecurity. But after all these years, I am very quick about thinking what I am thinking about. Dr. Audrey Chun of the Martha Stewart Center for Living at Mount Sinai Hospital says, "One of the factors in determining aging successfully is a resilient personality and the ability to recover from adversity and move on with life rather than dwell on challenges."

> Dwell: to linger over in thought or speech
>
> —Webster's Dictionary

We cannot hear enough how our ATTITUDES AFFECT our AGING. Yes, of course I cannot continue being busy all evening, like I used to be able to do. I know when I need to shut down. I need to monitor what I eat or do not eat, discipline myself to get out there and take that walk, or the consequences are far greater than when I was in my forties. I am in my early 70's now. What I choose to dwell on, regarding even my daily routine, has long and far-reaching effects on this aging body, and on my MINDSET and ATTITUDES. What I choose to dwell on will determine my day, my health, my relationships, and most definitely what my future will become. It has absolutely nothing to do with actual circumstances; but how I dwell on, or process, these aging circumstances that we all have, and we all evaluate one way or another. Do we give in to all of that negative thinking we have accepted as being compromised in our aging? Those with DESIGN SMARTS are fighting hard and will be the ones to not lose this battle. To many, this line of thinking will seem irrelevant; but to those going ahead of the pack with their DESIGN SMARTS ATTITUDES, the best is yet to come in a vibrantly exciting life.

If you listen very carefully, you will hear it and recognize this sound. It is called wisdom. Those with wisdom are not complainers, are not self-absorbed, but are the ones that are exciting and inspiring to be around. They enjoy their life by considering or thinking positively about what each day can bring in opportunities, whether being alone or with others.

I love what the late Robin Williams' character says in the movie Dead Poets Society: carpe diem. "Seize the day." Yes, this is it exactly. Those with DESIGN SMARTS are seizing each day to advance higher and higher in achieving an ageless and vibrant future. And for you too, if you choose to think about what you are thinking about; your future, and your life, will surely change for you and for those you love.

> "Men and women do not quit playing because they are old; they grow old because they quit playing."
>
> —Oliver Wendell Holmes

REFLECTIONS

1. Do you consider yourself to be open-minded when it comes to new ideas? Since your answer is yes, what specific attitudes in your home and your health will you plan to tweak?

   Home _____

   _____

   Health _____

   _____

2. How do you react when emotionally upset? Controlled response or normally out of control? Since all of us can always improve, what steps can you take to change your emotional reactions to emotional responses? _____

   _____

   _____

3. Excluding time with your family, do you filter who you spend time with on a regular basis?

                   YES   NO

4. Do you filter your social media contacts?

                   YES   NO

S.M.A.R.T.S.

 SPACES. Our spaces directly impact our lives. What is working in your home now? What is not?

 **MINDSETS.** Our lives directly follow our thinking. A positive mindset results in a positive life; a negative mindset results in a negative life. You get to choose.

 **ATTITUDES.** Our attitudes directly affect all and everything we do or become in our life. Age is just a number and you get to choose your attitude toward aging.

 **ROUTINES.** Our personal lifestyle in achieving wellness directly impacts our lives. Are you putting yourself first regarding your own personal life? You get to choose.

 **TOGETHERNESS.** Our relationships directly affect our quality of life. Giving back to your community and others changes everything. You get to choose to live outside of your inner circle connections.

 **SPIRITUAL.** Our personal decisions about spirituality affects our outlook on life. Everyone believes in something—either your own power or a divine power.

ROUTINES

IMPLEMENTATION PHASE

Chapter 12

Wellness Redefined: Health is the New Wealth

We All Want A Life of Wellness

Downsizing our ROUTINES gives us more time to cook and to eat healthy, to exercise, pursue hobbies, and live life unhurried. Very often our lives our full of unnecessary ROUTINES when analyzed reveal a lifestyle of mere busyness.

Another tidbit from my late dad: Without our health, we have nothing. Sound familiar? And from the extremely wealthy, late Steve Jobs: Without our health we are very poor. Health and Wellness is a topic trending everywhere as millions of Americans are dealing with, or are compromised by, various wellness issues. This is especially prevalent in the O50 demographic. Also, we can all relate that it seems like today, we have much more medicine, but much less health.

I believe that by living in the information overload world of today, there is a tendency to make wellness way more complicated than is really necessary to accomplish wellness goals. There are uncomplicated, basic, wellness principles that anyone, at any age, can incorporate into their lifestyle. If anyone believes that age compromises wellness, here is an example, out of the many, many thousands of examples, which emphatically disputes that age automatically diminishes the potential for wellness.

My mom at age 55, after retiring from a 25-year career at the Ohio Bell Telephone Company, started walking with her friends 5 miles a day. Yes, you read that correctly. And even more astonishing was that, unless it was icy or below 35 degrees, they were out there almost daily every week for years and years. Until she was in her late 80's, my mom had no heart issues and only took vitamins versus any prescription medications. Her uncomplicated wellness formula was healthy eating, drinking clean water, exercising, taking supplements, being a lifelong learner, plus regular medical and dental check-ups and age appropriate health testing. She was an energetic marvel to all who knew her and obviously was my greatest role model as an example for living a life of wellness. She might have been one of the first to understand that health is the new wealth.

What I still marvel at today was that my mom had and instinctively implemented sound common sense in her everyday lifestyle. She used to tell me, in no uncertain terms, when, in her opinion, I was neglecting my kid's health after I started working outside the home when they were in late grade school. When I would say, "Mom, I am too busy to cook like you do, and things are different today." Well, that was the wrong thing to say to a lady from the depression that took care of her brother's family of 3, due to the passing of her sister-in-law, plus her single brother, and my dad, my brother and me. I was reminded by her that there was no fast food, no dishwasher, and no automatic clothes washer and dryer. I vividly recall those conversations where she put in perspective how I was very, very spoiled. In my estimation, I was too busy and had to put my family's well-being aside. When the actual reality was, which she knew of course, that I could make the time, but I chose other ways to spend my time.

It's not that complicated. Keep it simple sister (or mister)!

Many people today feel overwhelmed when trying to figure out how to even begin to live a life of wellness. But in my humble opinion, it is not really all that complicated. I am not a complicated person in any areas of my life; so it stands to reason that my lifestyle is not very complicated either.

Have you ever observed people around you who are almost fanatical in their exercise routines, and yet eat so poorly? Or friends or family who brag about how little sleep they get, unlike the rest of us poor folks who admit to actually needing sleep and going to bed early? Have you ever heard experts explain how bad stress is for us, and yet they are way overweight? Of course, you have since it is everywhere. Sadly, most O50s have tunnel vision and often do not see the wholeness principle connected to all the facets needed to achieve a healthy lifestyle. I believe that very few accomplish total wholeness and balance every day. That is like saying, "I am perfect, and I do all things perfectly." The point is not perfection every single day. This is a self-defeating, hard to maintain perspective. I give it my all but most days I fall short in either controlling stress, eating healthy, getting a good night's sleep, or having R&R down time.

This is directing the focus to the everyday, normal person who is really trying to make a difference in their lifestyle routine. A key component is to know and accept the fact that life does indeed happen; and when it throws us off balance, we should not berate or belittle ourselves. We simply, without self- demoralizing guilt, recognize this unplanned detour and redirect ourselves when we can get back on track.

Living a life of wellness

Being a size eight or getting to the gym five days a week is not all there is to achieving wholeness. Let's dig deeper into this wholeness principle.

- Achieve balance
- Apply knowledge
- Prioritize you

These three principles are obvious, right? Except we must apply what we know; or quit fooling ourselves, like so many do, since they believe they already know all there is to know about their own wellness needs. This person is the hardest to motivate to change their lifestyle. A side note, or a thought here, is "why it is written that of the 7 deadly sins, the worst is pride?" By not receiving advice or guidance, pride can indeed be deadly when connected to wellness routines.

Who is taking care of you?

The third principle: PRIORITIZING YOU is also very clear. We cannot simply be all we are meant to be to others and ourselves if we do not make ourselves a priority! Who has the hardest time with this third principle? Well, it is women, of course! They almost gasp thinking, "How selfish are you Mitzi Beach to put yourself first? Why, that is the most self-centered, egotistical thing I have ever heard." Oh, really?

Then tell me this, dear ladies, who will take care of those you love and those you have responsibility for if you are not able to do so? Who will pay for your health and medical needs if you allow your health status to decline? And how loving can you be when you are so fatigued and overwhelmed from giving, giving, giving and never restoring "the you" in you?

Tell me again, who is being selfish, the woman who takes care of herself; or the woman who ignores her own needs? Most women put their needs on the "if I have time" part of their life-strangling to-do lists, and I am no exception. This is an area where I really struggle, not because I do not value my own self-care, but I allow other things often to crowd out what I need and should be doing.

So, we will journey together on achieving this life of Balance and Wholeness through these lifelong goals. And, for sure, they are to be our lifelong goals, not a flash in the pan, short-term emotional decision. Oh no, most certainly not, these goals are for our beautiful journey into the ultimate ageless vibrant life.

Eating habits

We all know what we should be doing to eat healthy, but here are a few more suggestions. What works for me is basically eating clean foods. These are just plain old "good for us"—nothing processed, little or no fast food, low salt, no bad fats, and organic when possible. But, remember, I am a foodie, so delicious and healthy are clearly not an oxymoron.

Eating habits greatly affect our weight, and controlling those pounds is essential in obtaining a life of wholeness and balance. We simply cannot be in balance being thirty to fifty pounds over our good, healthy weight. I know how hard this is! And getting older is no help either to keeping those pounds off. Nevertheless, the rewards totally "outweigh" the continuing weight war battles. Of course, all O50s already know this fact; the challenge is in the doing, to APPLY THE KNOWLEDGE. Isn't that true for all of life?

Exercise

Get moving! I heard a truly disturbing statistic recently that retirees watch six to eight hours of TV a day! Holy Cow! If some O50s retire in their mid-fifties and live to their mid-eighties, that's an immense amount of wasted time. This includes watching sports, weather, news, and the like; but still, how much of life is being compromised by this one fact alone?

The type of exercise is as important as exercising itself. Weight-bearing exercise for bone health, aerobic exercise for heart health, and yoga, Pilates, or the like for our physical balance—all are necessary to achieve the optimum life of health and wholeness.

I personally love walking outside, which is my weight-bearing routine, and most walks are aerobic. I also love yoga for stretching and balance. But here, also, I simply need to do more of both, which is my intention. We all know what road is paved with good intentions, right?

Maintaining our body posture is a biggie, and doing exercise makes us more and more aware of our posture—this is another area I have to keep working hard on. As we age, it is so easy to slouch instead of forcing our muscles to work by putting those shoulders back, lifting our head up, and tucking in that tummy. Stand up straight and be proud of who you are and how you look. It will definitely make a difference in your self-esteem. Try it and you'll see for yourself.

Besides the gym or a personal trainer, there are so many options for us to get exercise. Swimming, walking, biking, or exercise DVDs work wonders. I love doing my yoga DVD from the late Flora Edwards who way into her late eighties was our iconic yoga teacher at many venues throughout Wichita, Kansas Find something you love. Or maybe that is too strong an emotion for some of you regarding your exercise. Perhaps find something you at least enjoy and are willing to do!

Balanced Living

Of all the areas to wholeness, living a balanced life is where I hear the most lamenting about how to do it. With so many demands today on lives that seem to be busier than ever, how do we really ever achieve the ultimate balance in life?

I only know that I would be lying through my teeth if I professed to lead a balanced life. Here again, I am doing tons better, but I have a long way to go on these areas of achieving balance, which are:

Adequate sleep

A sleep study by the Center for Disease Control found that thirty percent of the US working population, or about 40 million Americans, get less than six hours of sleep a night. Another poll by the National Sleep Foundation indicated forty-five percent get less than seven hours of sleep each night. That's more than just a lot of sleepy people, as inadequate sleep robs us of our immune systems and our health.

Adequate sleep results in:

- Fewer aches and pains.
- Better moods and emotional stamina.
- Sharper thinking and ability to focus.
- Ease in maintaining weight.
- Increased memory recall.

Sleep is not just a luxury for when we have the time, but a serious need in our quest for better health, not to mention our quality of life. We know now that a good night's sleep is a big factor in our longevity, which makes perfect sense if we look at the above list.

> "Early to bed, early to rise,
> makes a man healthy, wealthy and wise."
> —Benjamin Franklin

Controlling Stress

I have written many blog posts on this subject, and there is no end in sight to what we are learning on the negative and life-draining effects of stress. One of the most significant advances in our medical pursuit of the whys of disease is, you guessed it correctly if you said, stress. And one of the main underlying culprits of stress in our lives is that it physically causes inflammation. Many medical professionals believe the inflammation that stress causes, is directly linked to heart disease, diabetes, cancer, arthritis, and other serious and chronic diseases.

When stress-induced inflammation occurs in our bodies, our cortisol levels increase, which is not a good thing. What was once commonly called the fight or flight syndrome, an increase in adrenalin so our bodies can kick into high gear in times of real danger or real crisis, is now how many people live on a day-to-day basis. Again, plain old common sense tells us that, eventually, we are going to wear ourselves out living in this state or pattern. But in today's crazy world, it is not only assumed that we are going to be on call 24-7, it is expected.

This is where I throw in the towel. I am not a machine. I do not and will not be available 24-7 for whoever feels their needs are so important that I am negligent if I do not respond on their timetable. This is a huge step for me, and especially one like me who is a recovering people pleaser. I will give my all during my defined working hours, giving and being all that I can possibly be to contribute, influence, or assist others. But when my day is over, it is over. And you know what? I am not the least bit guilty about it!

Of course, life issues happen, and of course for a very few key people and my precious family and grandchildren, I am open 24-7. But that is as far as I am willing to sacrifice my health in maintaining my balance of shutting down and turning off and tuning out.

But correcting our lifestyle ROUTINE is so much more difficult than taking a pill, right? You see we are still in the MINDSET that getting high blood pressure medicine, often caused by stress, or meds for the type 2 diabetes often caused by being very overweight, or meds for arthritis often caused by lack of exercise, or other issues taking meds is the only answer. Our "take a pill" mindset allows us to continue to function as we always have and is for the most part our medical way of life, or our path to health in America today.

I do not believe this is the way it has to be. And I do not live my own life this way. My first line of defense is to ask what can I do differently to avoid all these medical ailments, and if they occur, what life changes can I make to avoid taking meds? This is all part of the formula for being proactive in seeking our Balance and Wholeness.

Balance and Wholeness is, assuredly, the key to unlocking those doors to walking in the ultimate O50 power of living a healthy life. Just even thinking of the word "wholeness" gives the impression of nothing missing, nothing broken. Only with sincere introspection into our lives will the out-of-balance areas be revealed. Take the time to discern and process if your life is lacking balance like your life depends on it; because it surely does.

O50 wellness DESIGN SMARTS is all about wholeness...not perfection. It is about being healthy and not about being a size eight or getting to the gym five days a week. Oh no, it is much more involved for optimum wholeness and wellness in achieving the ultimate life.

A Life of DESIGN SMARTS—Wholeness & Wellness includes:

- Having healthy eating habits (chapter 14).
- Engaging in an exercise routine.
- Living a balanced life.
- Including time for social TOGETHERNESS.

Exercise Check list

- Weight-bearing exercise, such as walking, to maintain bone strength and bone health; lifting weights.
- Aerobic exercise that gets the heart rate up, such as swimming.
- Exercising at least three or four times weekly, incorporating weight-bearing and aerobic-type exercises.
- Stretching exercise, such as yoga or Pilates.
- Exercise for improved balance.
- Exercises to Improve posture.

Living a Balanced Life ~ The Ultimate O50 Challenge

- Time alone for unwinding.
- Get seven to eight hours of sleep a night.
- Control stress by whatever mentally or emotionally detoxifies you.
- Learn to recognize the "crazies" in life and how to deal or not deal with them.
- Take time just for yourself without feeling guilty.
- Take mental health days off.
- Find something that gives you joy and do it.
- Find your passion or hobby.

- Value yourself enough to schedule time for what needs you have, such as a massage.
- Spend time with those you love, such as family or friends.
- Stay connected socially.
- Allow for free time during the day, not scheduling yourself so tightly. Have some margin in your days.

REFLECTIONS

Reflect on your current wellness status. Please remember this is for your benefit and yours only so be brutally honest with yourself.

Where or how would you rate yourself? _____

_____

_____

What areas need improvement? _____

_____

_____

What is your specific personal improvement plans toward Wellness? ____

_____

_____

Remember, dear fellow O50, life is made up of choices. What you choose to do or incorporate today will absolutely affect what or how you look and feel five years from now.

Go for it! Live and enjoy the life that you were meant to have and live. If you do, your next years can definitely be your best years.

CHAPTER 13

Simple Routines versus Complicated Plans

DESIGN SMARTS comes with the understanding that healthy aging is 75% lifestyle, 25% genetics.

A few of the following statistics are being repeated in this section on Routines since they definitely affect the wellness of the O50 demographic. In the preparations to experience the best possible future, it is necessary to acknowledge the impact that millions of O50s have had, and will continue to have, on the American demographics. There is already a name for it called the "Silver Tsunami".

According to a panel of experts at the Aging in America Conference even way back in April 1, 2013, it was reported that the O50s (labeled Boomers) and the following demographics face both opportunities and potential crises. By 2020, the population of Americans age 55 to 65 will have grown an unprecedented 73% since 2000. According to Whole Living Magazine: "Anyone who thinks the boomers will turn 65 and be the same as the generation before are missing out on the last 60 years of sociology. The boomers change every stage of life through which they migrate." The boomers and those groups that follow will, and are, putting a huge strain on entitlement programs like Social Security and Medicare. In 2010, 39 million Americans received Social Security benefits. This was before the oldest of the Boomers turned sixty-five and became eligible and mandated to receive Medicare benefits.

By 2020, 64 million people will be eligible for Medicare, a whopping one-third more than in 2010. What troubles the experts is whether we have enough people in the younger generations to contribute working capital into these systems? Census takers reveal a big "no," since many will be minorities trying to achieve a higher standard of living as our American landscape changes. This is not a political commentary, but pure mathematical data that affects all the O50s.

I feel so passionate regarding the absolute necessity of getting these facts known to this huge demographic that will be affected in their health care benefits beyond what any of the experts can possibly predict. Sadly, however, is the certainty that it will not be a pretty sight. "Chronic disease is the single biggest driver of health care costs," says Dr. Rhonda Randall, chief medical officer of United Healthcare. And sixty percent of those over sixty-five live with one or more chronic diseases, such as diabetes and heart disease. Dr. Randall says that insurers are working to better coordinate care so that seniors stay healthy longer. I say and believe that is a good thing, but we need to be the ones trying to stay healthier longer by our lifestyle ROUTINE.

Do not buy the lie!

Know your enemy. Those equipped with DESIGN SMARTS understand that for, unfortunately, too many people, their enemy is apathy. However, those with DESIGN SMARTS will slay this enemy by caring, learning, and implementing a wellness lifestyle. More and more wellness information supports that our lifestyle ROUTINE is the only possible hope for securing a healthy future and, not health as a result of our genetic background, as formerly assumed. This is so critically important that, to repeat, research doctors and experts no longer believe a genetic predisposition to be an inevitable determining factor for our future health. It is all about our lifestyle routines.

This AMA backed research, reporting that lifestyle is more pertinent than genetics in affecting one's wellness potential, causes an uncomfortable response for many to acknowledge. I can hear the shouts regarding how such predispositions, such as a cancer gene, are certainly parts of one's genetic makeup. Of course, this knowledge is understood and assumed. But the lifestyle effect on our health cannot be disputed, especially since well over thirty percent of Americans are not only considered overweight, but obese. This one fact alone has far reaching consequences on one's wellness far beyond their genetic makeup. Factor in smoking, excess drinking of alcohol, no exercise, plus a sedentary life style; it becomes a challenge to purely blame one's genetic heritage for their wellness issues. Okay, I better stop now…

My personal silver tsunami

My personal tsunami episode occurred with one phone call out of the blue. Arlene Evans-Debeverly, an exceptional PA and national expert in women's health issues, called me herself and said; "I want to see you in my office at eight o'clock tomorrow morning." It takes months to get in to see Arlene, so that fact alone said something was up and it probably was not good news. And it wasn't. Bob went with me to this appointment to hear Arlene say that, if I fell off a bike or was injured in a car accident or any other of life's unplanned accidents, I could be in a wheel chair for the rest of my life. What??? Me???

This was such shocking news since I have been ultra-dedicated in taking care of my health for many years. Obviously, something was very wrong with my ROUTINE that was putting me at such risk. The tests revealed osteoporosis, the silent killer, which for me definitely was silent since I had no idea of this condition.

I must share that this was not my first bone density test known as a Dexa. However, at my post-menopausal age, my numbers took a dive from formerly being osteopenia to the full-blown osteoporosis. I learned that my personal profile of being from an Eastern European background, small framed with light eyes and skin, and not taking natural, bio-identical hormone supplements during menopause, contributed to my full-on osteoporosis bone density status. However, many, many women with just the opposite personal descendant profiles from mine are also dealing with this condition. It is surmised that thousands either do not know their bone density numbers or do not know how to fight osteoporosis vigorously.

This is where I cannot even express how critically important it is to be under the care of the right medical professional. Gone are the days for women to assume that any medical professional is an expert on their particular health risk. It is essential to be proactive concerning health care by doing homework on researching doctors and asking respected other women their advice in order to obtain the proactive up-to-date treatments. Find them! Don't be a nice little person who says, "Okay, give me the meds that everyone else is taking" without researching all options on any given health issue. Fight like your life depends on it because, it does!

Suffice it to say that Arlene spent a lengthy time with Bob and me showing us models of bone and what happens in the good bone versus the bad bone. This was an incredible, but scary, demonstration of where my bones were and why she was so majorly concerned about my future health. Her knowledge, experience and expertise, however, were what formed my lifestyle ROUTINE for my future by explaining the most commonly acceptable and most prescribed treatment. A trial period showed that this was not going to be aggressive enough for my osteoporosis numbers to improve.

Arlene's knowledge and experience, and most of all, her heart and motivation literally allowed me to get my life back to living without the

Simple Routines versus Complicated Plans

scary threat of osteoporosis. She explained and prescribed a very new medication available in Europe, but only recently approved in America. I took injections daily for two years with remarkable success. Now, I am on a treatment program of twice-a-year injections with my recent Dexa scan showing absolutely no osteoporosis or even osteopenia. A major point in revealing my health history is to emphasize that only by getting medical tests was I empowered to go to battle for my personal wellness future. Osteoporosis, and many other health risks, are obviously only determined by medical tests. Why then would anyone not have these tests? Understanding that many medical insurance plans do not cover all tests at all ages, there are, however, options available; but it takes a proactive commitment to find those resources.

Prevention, not medicine, is the key to wellness

My health battle was on big time because I was absolutely not going to just accept this bone density report and change my very active lifestyle to accommodate some stupid diagnosis. Being a firm believer in the power of prevention, I set out to learn, and then do all I possibly could, to not simply manage a diagnosis; but, to the best of my ability, get rid of it. And that is exactly what happened. Am I currently being naively arrogant assuming I have no health risks? Of course, I am not denying my need for medical tests as needed and many other daily lifestyle routines essential to my future wellness. And change my daily ROUTINE, I certainly did by learning that eighty percent of Americans are deficient in Vitamin D, which is essential for calcium absorption. I took a very high amount of prescribed Vitamin D for three months and was tested again, showing my numbers had indeed climbed to the correct level. I can happily share that my health today is excellent. I can also share that my health status is not merely by chance, but by diligently choosing to work as hard as I possibly can to maintain my wellness.

We O50s changed everything in America forever. So why would we not rebel against the most important issue of our lives, our own health?

I am a very private person regarding my health as my family and friends annoyingly will attest. For me to share this, and other of my health issues in the coming chapters, please know it is definitely not in my comfort zone to share what I believe is personal and private. My sole purpose is to emphasize, as strongly and as passionately as I possibly can, the major importance of doing whatever is necessary to achieve and maintain the best level of wellness conceivable.

I sadly hear so many people saying, "my arthritis" or "my back" or whatever is acting up. I say kick that "whatever" in the butt and do something about it! I will never be convinced that there is never ever any hope and that a diagnosis is just a concrete decree that must be accepted as body's age. We O50s changed everything in America forever. So why would we not rebel against the most important issue of our lives, our own health?

After two years of medical treatments, supplements, specific exercises, and diet, along with my natural hormone replacement therapy, my bone density numbers were remarkably positive, and my aggressive treatment was actually working! Wow, more proof to me that even if we have a bad report; we don't just talk about it, worry about it, or accept that report. We take the bull by the horns and believe that we can overcome high

Simple Routines versus Complicated Plans

blood pressure, pre-diabetes, aches and pains from arthritis, and other conditions. How? By changing our ROUTINES and seeking DESIGN SMARTS from whatever source we can. Again, we are in the information age, so lack of knowledge or lack of DESIGN SMARTS is simply not the way to fight back and is not an excuse.

Obviously, these beliefs of mine and zillions of other O50s, who are now fighting hard to age better and age smarter in America, are in no way meant for medical advice. Pure and simple, my only purpose is to wake up the savvy O50s to arm them with the fighting power that comes from getting the life empowering SMARTS. Why would we want any less for ourselves, and why wouldn't we want to be our best for all those we love and care about?

Every single choice you make definitely affects those in your personal or professional circle. For example, if you get enough sleep in your lifestyle ROUTINE, you are totally a different person than when you do not. In all areas of wholeness, like controlling stress, eating right, getting exercise, etc., living the life in daily ROUTINES not only gives the best to our life but to all those we care so deeply about because we cannot give away what we do not have.

I absolutely believe in the thousands who will indeed fight this battle of aging in America. They will do so with such gusto that all will know and see the results of their empowering lifestyle ROUTINES giving them a life others only envy from afar. By choosing to equip themselves with the DESIGN SMARTS or with other resources available, they are enabled to experience the ultimate vibrant life regardless of their age.

To those on the sideline of life, start fighting and fight hard to be all you were meant to be in your health, with renewed energy and a zest. Begin seizing new adventures and opportunities that are waiting for you to experience. I believe you can do it, and if you believe this too, watch out, your world will never be the same.

"Aging is accelerated by a lack of exercise. If you don't regularly exercise, you increase your risk for almost every kind of disorder, including heart disease, diabetes, arthritis and osteoporosis."

—The Mayo Clinic on Healthy Aging

Simple Routines versus Complicated Plans

REFLECTIONS

1. The medical world validates that the future of your health results from 75% lifestyle and 25% genetics. What, if any, genetic medical history have you assumed you were destined to develop? ___

   _____

   _____

2. Even though you may have the propensity for developing a genetic medical issue, what lifestyle changes can you implement to thwart this family medical history? _____

   _____

   _____

3. Are there medical diagnostic tests that you have not scheduled or have had yet? If so, please list these tests. Example: A colonoscopy.

   _____

   _____

   _____

CHAPTER 14

Easy Eating and Cooking Plans with Design SMARTS

Downsizing for wellness not only involves eliminating the unhealthy ROUTINE habits, but equally as important is eliminating the myths of healthy eating and cooking.

In this chapter, I am going to reveal exactly what I routinely cook, plus what I eat 80% of the time. But first I will attempt to *downsize* or reduce the myths relating to weight gain and our wellness status for the O50s. I must admit that this section of wellness is very challenging for me to write about due to my extreme awareness that one's personal weight status is just that, it is very personal! Again, please know and understand my heart is only motivated by my utmost desire to arm you with the realistic facts, not let you live by the untrue myths and unrealistic expectations. This chapter is tough love at its most potent example, and I expect to receive criticism for being too harsh. But I am willing to put myself out there for the good of the cause in the hopes that someone, somewhere, will wake up and change the direction of their lives. So here we go!

The acceptance of false aging beliefs can be very comforting for those overweight O50s who are accepting their status as just part of all those other awful and so-called facts about aging. Human nature routinely wants to take the path of least resistance. This can be disastrous if these aging lies are accepted by the millions of O50s are experiencing poor health. Over one third of Americans are considered obese and sadly again, this number is expected to rise due to many factors the least of all is ignorance of the facts.

Don't You Be One of Those to Buy These Very Common Lies!

- **LIE:** It is normal to lose energy as we age.
  ANTIDOTE: Exercise routinely, 7-8 hours of sleep per day, healthy eating, drink plenty of water.

- **LIE:** All my friends are taking statins or blood pressure medicine or are overweight. That's just the way it is at our age.
  ANTIDOTE: Exercise routinely, 7-8 hours of sleep per day, healthy eating, drink plenty of water.

- **LIE:** At my age, why does it matter anymore what I eat or look like?
  TRUTH: It will eventually have negative consequences on my family and the O50s community who will lose out if I am compromised in anyway.

- **LIE:** Nobody is cooking very much today.
  TRUTH: We love conveniences and many people either don't plan or are too lazy to make the effort

- **LIE:** I am too busy to cook.
  TRUTH: If you don't plan, you *are* too busy to cook. But if you plan, anyone can cook.

- **LIE:** It is just me or just the two of us so why bother?
  TRUTH: You make two people unhealthy rather than just one. Love your spouse/partner enough to make the effort to get both of you healthy.

- **OVERALL ANTIDOTE:** Study this entire chapter.

The sole purpose of this chapter is to shake up and spit out all those lies regarding aging in America today. And furthermore, this chapter is definitely not in any way meant to shame or lecture. That is absolutely not my intention! The purpose of this chapter is to give hopeful inspiration that these false paradigms, on what aging is and looks like, can be thoroughly disputed by my own personal life examples of wellness struggles. Plus, there are currently zillions of other O50s who are busting these aging misconceptions by refusing to listen any longer to the negative naysayers who unfortunately are accepting that these aging pounds, along with no energy, are simply part of normal aging. Wrong, wrong, wrong!

I will admit, however, that every decade does indeed make it harder to maintain a healthy weight. I am not disputing this constant challenge. But what I am disputing is that this ever-challenging weight gain associated with aging, must be accepted and tolerated as a given or understood as a reality of aging. To this thought, I say hogwash!

My Daily Routine

There are two main reasons why these personal revelations are being included in this book. The first reason is, in my 50's, I had to figure out a sensible and doable pattern to keep extra weight off my body. Frustratingly, now being in my 7th decade, the challenge continues to get harder and harder to keep a healthy weight. The first reason I am sharing, my insider secrets, is to bust that mistaken belief that I am just one of those lucky people that can eat whatever they want and never gain a pound. Unfortunately, my weight is not only a constant challenge, but also when the pounds come on; they become more difficult and harder to get rid of with each passing year.

The second reason for sharing my personal eating and cooking routine is to bust the thousands of lies about what aging does to our weight as we age. More importantly, however, is to bust the lies that many people *want* to believe about gaining weight as they age. Why is this the case?

I am prepared to also get a lot of criticism regarding this first shared routine of mine. I weigh myself every single morning before I eat or drink anything. I can hear the gasps and see the eyes rolling! This works for me now, and has for years and years, and I will explain why this has been so helpful to keep me wearing skinny jeans. I am not obsessive about weight, or a fanatic about being model thin. But I do have a small frame so extra weight on me goes to very unattractive places like a bulging tummy and flabby, large thighs. Those extra pounds could be easily hidden by wearing large loose tops or even buying several pairs of different sized jeans to have for those good days and for those fat days. But what does this accomplish in the end other than accepting those extra pounds? Unfortunately, almost everyone has experienced gaining this extra weight that normally turns into accepted pounds and larger loose tops. By the time this happens, the discouragement is so high that giving up and buying the lies is just so much easier.

Most days, I have a plan for that entire day of eating.

This is why I weigh myself every morning. If I am a few pounds over my normal weight, then I compare those unwanted pounds to being overdrawn in my checking account with penalty fees ahead. Ignoring my "overdraft" will inevitably result in higher and higher fees. It could result in the bank shutting down my account due to my irresponsible financial behavior. to eat for the coming day. This habit constantly reveals to me the cause and effect of my eating consumption from the day before, giv-

Easy Eating and Cooking Plans with Design SMARTS

ing me a heads up for the day ahead. Many say that if their clothes are too tight, then they know it is time to cut back. But for me, this is my plan and it works like a charm. Is it easy? Of course not, but is anything in life that is going against all odds ever easy?

I have had a love affair with food for as long as I can remember. I am one of those people who live to eat and not eat to live. Without a doubt, I am a foodie. Meaning I enjoy delicious food and rarely, if ever, eat foods that are simply available to me, but are not tasty. This will also be a shock to most people, but I think about my upcoming meals every day. Most days, I have a plan for that entire day of eating. The majority of my friends cannot believe that is how I maintain my weight; but also, it is assuredly how I maintain good health. I never take my health for granted, strongly believing that it is my responsibility to eat the best I can to be all that I can possibly be. The adage that "we are what we eat" could not be more applicable than how our daily eating is managed. If, then, we are a walking billboard of what we did or did not do five years earlier; doesn't it make sense to get serious about our eating?

In addition to eating as healthy as I can, I take a ton of health supplements. I know I know that, ideally, we should get our nutrition from our food. I certainly agree that is the goal. However, this statement, to me, shows a lack of knowledge regarding our farming practices of today. It would take many, many cups of spinach, for example, to reap the nutrition benefits that one cup of spinach had decades ago. This is the result of overzealous farming techniques that have depleted the soil and compromised the nutritional value of many of our foods. Adding to this thought of receiving the necessary nutrients from our food, I would like to know how many of us every single day have all the recommended servings of fruits, vegetables, protein, dairy, fiber, or whole grains. Even as hard as many of us try to do daily, this simply is not a reality for most of us. I am especially frustrated when I hear doctors pronounce supplements as a total waste of money. In reality, most doctors have maybe one semester of nutrition in their medical training.

I have a plan for what Bob and I will eat for at least a few days and schedule my trip to the grocery store to buy what is needed. Like everyone else, I am way too busy to be running to the store every day. We are also really good at eating leftovers, so cooking a pot of soup or grilling lots of chicken breasts works great for us, especially on our busy days. In order to eat healthy, I believe that there must be a plan to have the food in the house that is needed for the plan, to avoid stopping at fast food or grabbing junk food for dinner.

I would guess that this next particular routine of mine is also unique, perhaps unusual, but it keeps me going at the top of my game. I eat 3 meals daily. Through trial and many errors, what works best for my physical requirements are breakfast, lunch, and dinner, but the key is what I eat. I also am a huge believer in a mid-afternoon healthy snack, if low level energy attacks me, which it normally does. Engines require fuel to run exactly like the human body requires. I marvel at people who do not eat breakfast or anything at all until lunchtime. This goes against the theory that our body's metabolism is activated by food. Therefore, I believe eating three meals daily turns us into lean, mean, food burning machines.

The biggest obstacle, in maintaining my weight and energy, is without a doubt getting enough exercise. There are, not so pretty, physical body consequences as well when my exercise routine is reduced or when I am unable to make exercise happen at all. Being busy is no longer an excuse for me. The reality of my life is that I am always going to be busy. This is just how I roll. I love it, but I must figure out a better plan to keep this O50 going at top speed by having a no excuse exercise commitment.

My easy, fast, healthy cooking philosophy

The essential element of DESIGN SMARTS is cooking healthy, fast, and delicious food. I am not a complicated cook at this stage of life. About 80% of the time I cook healthy and nutritious meals. Rarely do I prepare meals that take a lot of prep time or are highly fattening. But as most know, in my 80-20 philosophy, 20% of the time there's chicken parmesan or other high calorie foods cooking in my kitchen for my family or friends. One of the biggest obstacles in cooking is know how to cook easy, healthy, and delicious meals.

There are tons of cooking sites on line and numerous TV networks like *The Food Channel*. But for most people, there remains this dilemma of how to get it done for themselves. especially with such busy lives we have today. My answer is easy, simple and fast; think ahead of time what's for dinner and have a plan. Anyone can bring home a cooked rotisserie chicken and a salad from the salad bar when there is simply no time to cook. Or one can stop at Whole Foods, or similar food stores, to select a healthy protein and a vegetable side dish. Here is a basic run down of how I cook for me and Bob.

My DESIGN SMARTS cooking tips

1. The first thing I determine in planning for dinner is what is the source of protein? I cook a lot of salmon or tilapia, lean beef and pork, and, of course, chicken. Mastering how to quickly cook seafood on the stove is one of my easiest, fastest, and healthiest ways to do a dinner.

2. Side dishes are often steamed broccoli or other fresh vegetables. I keep frozen vegetables on hand at all times in the freezer for when there is no time to get to the store. But I never microwave vegetables, regardless of common practices today. Way back in

my nutrition classes at Ohio University, I learned that microwaves destroy many of the enzymes present in vegetables. Again, I know this will be debated, but as aging occurs, so does our ability to maintain digestive enzymes essential for good digestion. I continue do what I do and feel no obligation to defend my mindset.

3. For jazzing up any main dish, side dish or salad, keeping strong cheese flavors on hand like feta or parmesan can add just the needed flavor punch for satisfying even plainly cooked proteins or vegetables. The key here is to add a pinch not tons of cheese that can or will offset the healthy eating and calorie count. I love adding fresh lemon juice and olive oil to my seafood, spinach or broccoli. There's often a pinch of garlic added to my cooking, as well as lots of herbs for flavor, versus tons of cheese or other high calorie options.

4. Since I learned to read and understand what is in most bottled salad dressings, I make my own, which is so easy and uncomplicated. A good oil, like avocado or olive oil, with an acid like a flavored vinegar, lemon or orange juice, add a little salt and pepper and an herb of choice and done. By being healthier and definitely cheaper, and so easy, making a fresh salad dressing is a DESIGN SMARTS favorite.

5. Please forgive me for not adding more recipes but my cooking is based on the philosophy that I have given you and not by exact recipes. My healthy cooking is really so basic and so very easy! I have however, added a few since this has been requested plus that I do webinars on how easy and fast my healthy cooking really is to accomplish.

Easy Eating and Cooking Plans with Design SMARTS

The reality of the O50 health status today and how to avoid these pitfalls

There are 73 million O50s, and most are too tired or too busy to cook. Whether we want to admit it or not, knowing what to cook is our biggest obstacle. It is not that we do not want to eat healthier. It is choosing to create or develop a new MINDSET to change old patterns of eating and cooking that is the true crux of this problem. Do you know that it takes over 8 times of repetition to form a new habit? Plus, it takes even more times to reverse an existing habit; so it is imperative to realize that learning to eat and cook healthier is a process. No pun intended, but don't try to consume this new lifestyle of eating and cooking healthy in one bite. We are so hard on ourselves that if we mess up, we often want to give up. But hang in there and keep on "keeping on" even if it means only one time a week you choose to not grab and eat; but instead cook a healthy meal at home. Then, the next week, go for 2 meals. Be intentional in your choices and you will be DESIGN SMART.

> "The foods we eat have an enormous impact on our health, our well-being and even our mood. In that sense, food has incredible power: the power to increase and sustain energy: the power to heal."
>
> —Whole Living Magazine (Power Foods)

This is my normal daily food and drink intake

Hopefully, for most of you, this section will not be TMI. My only reason for giving my eating routine is that I have been asked so many times what I eat daily. Therefore, I would feel remiss to not include my routine in this chapter. So here is my DESIGN SMARTS daily eating plan.

I am an early bird often rising at 5:30 am to maximize my highest level of thinking, creating, and writing at this time of the day. I start this beautiful dawn time with a cup of coffee, with half and half, and one piece of sprouted whole grain toast with natural almond or peanut butter. Before I have my actual breakfast, I drink a cup of warm water with one fresh squeezed lemon. Around 9:00 am, I have my normal breakfast of 2 eggs, another piece of the same toast, and another cup of DECAF coffee with half and half. Most days this holds me to lunch, but only if it's an early lunch. Being a major believer in keeping my blood sugar level up, I may need a mid-morning protein type snack.

Lunch is my hardest challenge, so I do a lot of tuna with a little olive/mayo combo and garlic salt or whatever protein is left over from dinner. Add a fresh apple or pear, and a piece or two of dark chocolate, and I am good to go. This is also why I cook a lot of soups and healthy stews to have for a quick and energy packed lunch.

Before dinner, on most days, Bob and I often have a happy hour together to catch up on the events of our day. It's a special treat to unwind with a nice glass of red wine before eating dinner at around sixish. Eating a late dinner (later than 6:30) doesn't work well for either of us for getting a restful night's sleep. One of the reasons I cook dinner almost every night is because it's one of the ways that I can spoil Bob, plus he totally appreciates my cooking and will eat just about anything, like the old Mikie commercial. Bob always does the grilling, which is just fine by me. Then, I only have to prepare a veggie or side dish. Our dinners are not fancy or complicated, with the majority of the time simply being a piece meat, fish, or chicken and a healthy side dish. A piece or two of dark chocolate after dinner does it for me for the day, and I very rarely eat anything in the evening after my chocolate.

As I have mentioned, I cook a lot of soups and stews often starting in my crockpot. Also, I love creating easy one pan meals. I start starting by browning Italian style ground turkey, adding canned organic diced tomatoes, herbs and spices and then adding tons of vegetables to steam with the cooked ground turkey.

I sincerely hope that you understand how truly easy it is to eat and cook healthy, seeing how simple and basic my eating and cooking style and philosophy is on a daily basis. Life often feels like it is on steroids, so adding more pressure with complicated eating and cooking plans makes no sense to me. Many of you may be asking, "How can you possibly eat and cook in a similar pattern as I do?" Because you have bought the lies and believe it is all just too time consuming and too darn hard to accomplish. Well, it is a matter of choice, isn't it? Could you choose to perhaps try a new pattern of eating and cooking? I must, again, reinforce to you how crazy busy my days and weeks are even now in my 70's. And yet, I have a plan and I choose to work this plan. I am in no way trying to be all knowing or even in the least bit condemning of your life choices.

My only motivation is that I want so badly for you to live a healthy, energetic, and vibrant life ahead. The wonderful thing is that it is totally up to you. It is only you who gets to choose to live a lovely life of your choosing by reducing your health risks; or you can gamble with your life by living a life of chance. I bet you know what I am hoping you choose.

# REFLECTIONS

1. From the first page of this chapter, what lies about aging have you accepted as gospel truth? Be honest, this is for your eyes only.

   _____

   _____

2. The nutrient value of today's food is often compromised. Since you acknowledge that every day you don't get the recommended vitamin and mineral requirement from the foods you eat, what supplements are you taking? What supplements can you research, for your particular age and physical needs, that you should be taking. _____

   _____

   _____

3. If your weight is not where you want it to be, what are you goals for weighing less? _____

   _____

   _____

MITZI'S EASY COOKING RECIPES

Festive Peppers Recipe

Please see video on www.mitzibeach.com

The designer in me loves the colors!

This is a very healthy, easy, fast, and low-fat yummy recipe that we love for the intense flavors, great texture. A green salad and hearty whole grain bread will complete the meal for sure.

Serves 4 Recipe doubles very well

1 1 # package Honeysuckle Mild Italian Turkey Sausage

3 fresh peppers cut into 2" long Julienne strips (I used 1each of yellow, orange, & red)

2 cans 141/2 ounces Hunts Diced Tomatoes + 1 can of water (I like having lots of broth for dunking bread)

2 tsp olive oil

1 T dried basil

2 tsp dried garlic flakes

1tsp dried oregano

1/2 tsp course ground pepper

Grated parmesan cheese for garnish (optional but I love adding it)

Brown turkey sausage in olive oil

Add dried & garlic, & spices

Add tomatoes + water

Then the peppers

Cover and simmer on medium to low heat for 20 - 30 minutes. Let sit about 15 min or longer for flavors to absorb while finishing dinner prep. Great reheated!

Jewish Penicillin Soup

In honor of my many Jewish friends who taught me valuable lessons on eating well, I share with you one of my favorites.

2 chicken breasts

2 cups water

8 cups chicken broth

4 carrots cleaned and chopped

4 stalks of celery+ leaves cleaned and chopped

1 small onion or 1 Tablespoon dried onion

1 tsp black pepper

1 tsp salt

1 pkg frozen peas

1 pkg frozen spinach

t tsp dried basil leaves

1 Tablespoon balsamic vinegar

garlic salt to taste

parmesan cheese optional garnish

Place cut up chicken breast in water and broth with carrots, onion, celery, salt and pepper and cook for 45min on low heat or simmer

Cup chicken into smaller pieces if necessary. Add frozen or fresh vegetables and remaining ingredients and simmer for 30 -45 minutes

Check seasonings

Freezes beautifully

Can use chicken or turkey stock from cooking chicken or turkey bones from either store bought roasted leftover chicken or leftovers from any meal.

Any vegetables whether fresh or frozen work beautifully in this soup and the more vegetables the healthier the soup. This is why this is called Jewish Penicillin Soup on Steroids! (I added the "on Steroids.")

Kick Butt Soup... My Secret Weapon!

I love soup. I make soup. I create new soups.

And I believe soups are one of our most effective weapons for the battles of fighting flu and colds, getting easy nutrition fast, a huge weapon for me on weight control, and can be cooked ahead for MANY meals.

But, the big BUT in my kick butt soups are :

Do not use processed foods like canned mushroom or chicken...yuck, yuck yuck!

No white pasta or white rice, white sugar. You get the idea.

Or using tons of cheese or not draining fat off hamburger before adding to soup.

Very rarely do I ever make or eat a cream soup normally loaded with butter & cream ...that is so not going to accomplish any of the attributes listed above. Yummy...Yes! Healthy...no!

But remember, I do live by my 80 - 20 rule and if I want some broccoli cheese soup, well, then, I factor that into my 20% and enjoy it to the max!

Normally at least twice a month, I make some kind of soup and freeze some in single size servings for myself for lunch or dinner. Talk about comfort food and no mess or cooking! Truly feeds my tired soul many nights.

I have MANY variations of my Kick Butt Soup but the basics are:

I normally use chuck roast.

Using SHARP knife (my late dad used to say that the most dangerous thing is a dull kitchen knife), cut off as much fat as possible

I cut meat into chunks for faster slow cooker results and easier cutting up for soup.

For this soup, I added to crock pot left over red wine, (oxymoron?) 1 can Hunts natural diced tomatoes, garlic salt, pepper, and 2c of the water

I have used Lipton beefy onion mix but my "clean eating" conscious is struggling with this addition but I'm good...not perfect :)

Cook on high for 2 hours and 6 hrs on low or until meat is sooo tender. I let the slow cooker cool after done cooking, then refrigerate until the yucky artery clogging fat solidifies on the surface and skim it off. Remove the meat and shred or cut up bite size. Then add meat and broth to large soup pan.

Veggie options...unlimited!

Cabbage. onion, carrots, green beans, mixed veggies frozen, and at the end, fresh parsley and fresh spinach is my pick for this soup.

Cup up veggies and add to soup with additional canned tomatoes, water, & seasonings to taste simmer approximately 1 - 2 hours depending how done one likes their veggies

Last 1/2 hour, add fresh parsley and fresh spinach

Garnish with fresh parmesan if desired and enjoy...your body will be saying "thank you, thank you"!

Recipe (This is for soup so never an exact science to me)

Chuck Roast

Veggie Option:

cabbage, carrots, onions, mixed veg & green beans frozen, fresh parsley & spinach

(I often use a mixture of fresh or frozen veggies) or zucchini, leeks, kale, or whatever floats your little boat.

Hunts Natural Diced Tomatoes 2 - 3 cans

6 -8 cups water depending on amounts of veggie used. Remember this is soup. Not a science project!

1 cup red wine or sub with water

1/4 c dried minced garlic

1/2 tsp garlic salt & ground black pepper

and again, at final cooking soup mixture, garlic salt & pepper

1 tsp of basil & oregano or more to taste. I use more

Fresh parmesan to garnish optional

Mange' Enjoy!

Chapter 15

Can Your Furniture Sabotage Your Wellness?

Yes, *so downsize* your unhealthy, uncomfortable furniture now! "Oh, my aching back!" It's not only airline seats or poorly designed seats in our cars that can give us back pain. Most people are shocked to learn that our very own furniture can be the culprit causing our back pain. Furniture can definitely be the cause of back pain or can aggravate other wellness issues as well. Furniture can also cause stiff necks, shoulder pain, and headaches to name a few unwanted ramifications of buying or living with, the wrong or incorrect furniture that can indeed sabotage our individual health requirements.

Remember Archie Bunker's infamous recliner in the sitcom, "All in the Family?" Many jokes were made about that awful, beyond ugly recliner. But it is no joking matter if Archie's, or anyone else's recliner, is the root cause of anyone's unfortunate and unexpected back pain. Dr. Bryan Kamps of Spectrum Health in an article by Eve Clayton says, "If your recliner doesn't support your lower back, the chair could do your body more harm than good. To help your posture, add support by tucking a rolled towel or a small cushion against your lower back. If you're buying a new recliner, pay attention to what you feel at your lower back as you try out the options. If there's nothing there, it's probably going to make your back pain worse," he said. "Or if you don't have back pain, it's going to give you back pain."

In today's busy world, stress is a huge deterrent to anyone's wellness. Connecting the dots or paying attention to unsuspecting, but relevant, causes of physical stresses even in our own furniture is more than enough of a reason to evaluate what we sit on day in and day out, year after year, right? Especially for the O50s, inflammation due to stress, whether it be emotional or physical, is the underlying cause of many serious diseases facing millions of people. Therefore, this huge and powerful demographic of O50s is awakening to how their specific furniture purchases can promote and help them to experience greater wellness, function, and, of course, pizazz and style. Therefore, placing an extremely high priority on avoiding stress in our home life certainly makes another case for learning and implementing DESIGN SMARTS, even in furniture.

Healing spaces must have appropriate furniture

Have you considered how your furniture, lighting, or accessories promotes or hinders your health and wellness in your very own home?

Let's review and reiterate that 80% of our time spent at home is in 20% of our home's space excluding sleeping in the bedroom or time in the bathroom. This 80% time, in your most frequently used spaces, is where you are working on your laptops or mobile devices, eating, reading, watching TV, socializing, or just hanging out. Now ask yourself "Is this space truly comfortable and functional for you?" Yes, it really does matter if the furniture you sit in daily is appropriate for you and your overall wellbeing. This furniture that is used so often by you, if poorly designed or inappropriate for your body size, can have adverse results leading to neck, back, or shoulder pain and discomfort along with headaches. Therefore, DESIGN SMARTS can help you select furniture ergonomically proportioned for you and not the masses!

And if anyone should know better on how to select furniture for personal needs, surely it should be my personal furniture selections, right? Well, I certainly blew it for our Cypress home when I purchased a long sofa, instead of two chairs with ottomans for where we spend 80% of our time while relaxing or watching TV. My intent was to have more TV room for when our grandchildren visited which, of course, is super important. However, the majority of the time, it is only Bob and me. This example emphasizes my point. Do what works for the person who is sitting in the furniture the majority of the time. I am not comfortable relaxing on this sofa because it does not support my back, even after adding extra cushions. You are probably wondering why I selected this style of sofa in the first place, which is a legitimate question. I had actually sat in this sofa before buying so it wasn't as if I ordered an unknown style of sofa. But overriding my own personal design philosophy, I selected this particular sofa because I was thinking of others. As the late Ricky Nelson song, Garden Party, "I learned my lesson well." However, in our next last-nest-place, I carefully selected two chairs with ottomans for our 80% down time relax space. In another area will be sofas and other chairs for our family and friends; but for our extremely important time to chill, I did it right this time.

Steps to make your furniture work for you

With the appropriate furniture, wellness can be enhanced through these reasons:

- **Comfort** to provide for the restorative rest and relaxation essential to allow our bodies to recover needed by everyone.
- **Ergonomics to** nurture our physical needs with correct scale and proportion in seat depth, height of back cushions, and style of seat cushions.

- **Safety** within home traffic patterns by avoiding too much furniture. Overcrowded rooms inhibit safe passage leading to tripping over table legs and other deterrents.

What the O50s want in their furniture.

The O50s mean big business today for furniture retailers and interior designers according to the International Council of Shopping Centers (ICSC) and the Economic Policy Institute. This is because the O50 age group controls more than three-fourths of America's wealth and has three times the net worth of younger generations. Most importantly, this demographic outspends other generations by 400 hundred billion dollars each year on consumer goods and services, according to the U.S. Government Consumer Spending Survey. And yet I must again add, "they do not see us" as chapter 2 verifies.

Additionally, the immense purchasing power of this huge O50 demographic is still growing according to Forrester Research, "By 2025, one-fifth of the US population will be 65+. And surprisingly, Boomers outspend younger adults online 2:1on a per capita basis". But why is this data even remotely relevant for you? It justifies that you have requirements for what you need in your home life. There is power in this influence from the O50s that should be heard by furniture retailers and furniture designers. You deserve to have furniture options that will allow you to live more comfortably with less physical stress. And you certainly don't deserve a condescending attitude when asking for furniture options and features to meet your O50 needs.

Furniture features The O50s will be, seeking:

- A wireless charging oasis embedded in furniture.
- Affordable luxury in styles that fit scale and proportion requirements.
- Multifunctional Furniture.
- Motion furniture with swivel or glide options and furniture with moving parts and pieces like stackable tables.
- Inventive storage furniture.
- Technology built into furniture--like speakers in recliners, USB ports, or blue tooth features.
- Desks or work stations with stand-up computer features.

Furniture has more impact and potential than we realize

In the article, "The Transformative Power of Furniture,"i+D July/August 2018,the magazine of the American Society of Interior Designers and the Interior Designers of Canada, Lisa Blecker, director of marketing for Resource Furniture, states "Certain household typographies are under-served in the housing market. No one is building enough housing for these groups because they are somewhat under the radar, but they're all increasing dramatically, and they have very distinct needs within a home." She explains that there are three living groups with these needs. They are unrelated adults living together as roommates; multigenerational households-another hugely growing segment; and older people aging in place. She explains that, *by only changing the furniture, all three of these household scenarios could be served.*

This was demonstrated in an exhibition at the National Building Museum in Washington, D.C. titled Making Room: Housing for a Changing America. Of great value to consumers is her statement that the furniture used in this exhibit is not a prototype but is available today.

What potential possibilities then exist by knowing the impact of furniture's influence on our life stages and these various housing models of today.

Tips on what to look for when buying furniture and the reasons why

I am often astounded how extremely uncomfortable dining room chairs can be due to the incorrect **pitch of the back of the chair** (pitch is the vertical angle of the chair relative to the seat—normally it's angled back a little). This negative impact can be experienced on high-end furniture as well as the lower priced chairs. For this reason, before buying an entire set of chairs for your dining area, sit in the chair being considered. This is more than common sense; it is obviously imperative for everyone's comfort.

The pitch of any given side chair or dining chair is one of the few furniture pieces that does not depend on body size. Badly designed chairs with too straight of a pitch to the back of the chair, simply does not work for anyone. What's the answer if unable to "test drive a chair being considered?" It may sound radical to some but ordering one chair for evaluation has far more DESIGN SMARTS than ordering a set of chairs or barstools that end up being a disastrous and expensive selection mistake. It is essential to find out, before ordering anything not physically possible to sit in as a test, the manufacturer's return policy.

For over 3 decades, I have personally sat in more sofas and chairs at furniture markets than I can possibly count for the sole purpose of their comfort rating. Obviously, for sofas and club chairs versus a dining chair, this is a subjective opinion. Nevertheless, I can spot a red flag a long way off on poorly designed furniture in the comfort or ergonomic department. My clients have trusted me to be the design sleuth for their wellness and wellbeing and to be unquestionably truthful to them. I have been my client's furniture ambassador whom they have trusted. They know that I have carefully evaluated their furniture before one piece of furniture is ever ordered through my business. Beauty or design alone is often an unwise reason to purchase furniture.

But above all, everyone needs a comfy, nurturing chair or sofa—absolutely everyone.

The depth of the seat, whether it is a sofa, club chair, or any other furniture piece, is of extreme importance to meet the requirements of individual body types. How can someone over 6 feet tall be happily satisfied and comfortable in a chair or sofa designed for someone 5 feet tall. I have often asked total strangers, of different heights, at market to sit in a chair or ottoman for their evaluation to see if it is comfortable for them. It would be laughable, if not sadly so common, to see a shorter person's feet not even touch the ground because the depth of the seat is too deep. If trying to evaluate what works best for you, measure the depth of a chair or sofa that is particularly comfortable for you as a guide to compare this depth of furniture to what you are considering purchasing.

Use the experts available to up-an interior designer or a furniture store's consultant that you trust, to find what is best for your personal and individual needs in furniture pieces. It is, by far, money well spent versus the zillions of sad stories that I have heard over the years by my discouraged and unhappy clients that had previously purchased major mistakes in their furniture acquisitions. Perhaps, you can relate?

Seat and back cushion styles play a huge part in how any given sofa or chair works for the individual's comfort and ergonomic function. There are probably as many different cushion effects as there are styles of furniture and they all feel different to different people. Too soft or deep cushy seat cushions can make it extremely hard for those with any compromised health issues, or even without health issues, to gracefully stand up. But aside from this "stand up" issue; everyone wants their favorite chair or sofa to work for their "come home to momma" feeling when they can finally relax and sink into their own little corner of the world. So again, if you are unable to physically sit in furniture that is being considered for purchase, go to the experts for advice. This is using DESIGN SMARTS to avoid furniture buying mistakes. But above all, everyone needs a comfy, nurturing chair or sofa—absolutely everyone.

Arm rest styles often are selected solely on design preferences, but for the O50s, there is so much more to consider. For instance, too low or too high of arm styles are not ergonomically comfortable. And large, over scaled, rolled arms are a definite "no" because of the footprint they consume versus the actual seating space. Furthermore, this demographic does not necessarily know where they will live or who will be living with them.

Furniture expenditures, for most O50s, do not happen very frequently. This is the reason behind knowing all of these different, and albeit, confusing, options of furniture specifics before ordering or buying any furniture. As noted in this chapter, furniture can potentially change our living spaces and time spent in our home yielding personal benefit or constant aggravation, like a stone in our shoe. Exactly like so many other decisions in life, even though it is merely furniture, the consequences of hasty uninformed purchasing decisions can leave a bitter taste for a very long time. I want and wish for all of you to be a cut above the masses that so often impulsively go out and buy, or order, online furniture due to a sale or a spur of the moment, emotional decision. You are smarter than "those types of uninformed consumers"; you are a cut above the masses now because you proudly have DESIGN SMARTS on your side yielding ultimate life advantages, even in buying furniture.

REFLECTIONS

1. What specific furniture do you sit in most of the time to:

   Eat? _____

   Do laptop work? _____

   Relax or watch TV? _____

   How ergonomic for your back and your posture is this furniture?
   _____

2. Is your home busting at the seams with too much of everything spilling over everywhere? List items or furniture pieces in realistically just need to go. _____
   _____
   _____
   _____
   _____
   _____
   _____

S.M.A.R.T.S.

 SPACES. Our spaces directly impact our lives. What is working in your home now? What is not?

 **MINDSETS.** Our lives directly follow our thinking. A positive mindset results in a positive life; a negative mindset results in a negative life. You get to choose.

 **ATTITUDES.** Our attitudes directly affect all and everything we do or become in our life. Age is just a number and you get to choose your attitude toward aging.

 **ROUTINES.** Our personal lifestyle in achieving wellness directly impacts our lives. Are you putting yourself first regarding your own personal life? You get to choose.

 **TOGETHERNESS.** Our relationships directly affect our quality of life. Giving back to your community and others changes everything. You get to choose to live outside of your inner circle connections.

 **SPIRITUAL.** Our personal decisions about spirituality affects our outlook on life. Everyone believes in something—either your own power or a divine power.

TOGETHERNESS

ACCESSORIZING PHASE

CHAPTER 16

A Path to Joyful Living That's Not All About Me

Can you consider the thought that if you *downsized* the amount of time you spent on your own personal discretionary activities, you could have the time to give back to volunteer at perhaps Red Cross, church activities, or other community or individual needs? This story with my young granddaughter is a perfect example of TOGETHERNESS. She chose to use her rare and special time with me in Wichita to give back to someone else versus choosing this time for her own enjoyment

"But Mimi, you have to go back and get more flowers because the other residents all look so sad!" This, at that time, was my 14 year- old granddaughter emphatically begging me to return to Sam's to buy more flowers. It happened to be a 104-degree day in Wichita so getting inside my car again, with the inside temperature of about 120 degrees, was definitely not in my plans.

There it was hitting me smack dab in my O50 grandmother face, a perfect example of living for others. I was fine with buying the first batch of fresh flowers for my nursing home friend Lola, but when it meant that I was going to be uncomfortable going back for more, I resisted. Intuitively, Megan understood this principle by reminding me many times that, before we even went to see our dear Lola in the nursing home;

we simply had to take her flowers. Then she decided we had to buy lots of flowers for the others. So we purchased many bouquets to give out in the dining hall during lunch. But then we ran out of flowers. I tried very hard to convince Megan that it was okay, and we would do this again another time, but no way was she accepting this thought. Off I went to buy more flowers as Megan had a grand time wheeling 93- year old Miss Lola around the halls of the nursery home.

When I returned, they were both beaming and laughing at their insider jokes and having the best of times. Megan's joyful countenance, however, changed to one of sadness as we returned to the dining hall to hand out the additional flowers; but it was empty of the residents. I told Megan we could leave the flowers with staff to give out later. "No Mimi, I have to let them know that I didn't leave them out on purpose." So off we went, knocking on the resident's doors to give out the flowers. This young lady received an intangible, but lasting, reward that day by the look on those residents faces realizing that they too were getting a flower and were not forgotten.

It's not about me

The famous inaugural speech by President John F. Kennedy stated, "Ask not what your country can do for you, but ask what you can do for your country?" In this chapter, by connecting the dots of having an attitude of giving, I believe we can lead a joyful life for the O50s. This is not only about giving money. It is also about giving of oneself in ways that are totally unique to their individual gifts and talents.

Of course, I love all the chapters in my book. But if I were asked which chapter I believe will have the most profound effect on living a joyful life, I would have to say this chapter. To have passion or compassion, empathy, and a caring heart for others, to me, is the secret sauce to aging with not only a joyful spirit, but with a healthier mind and body as well.

Faith without works is meaningless. But works without a heart of love and compassion, to me, is equally as meaningless.

How pitiful it is to observe older, self-absorbed, overly sensitive, easily offended, complaining, O50s speaking only of themselves and their needs and their issues. These types of people rarely ask how others are doing because they are so engrossed in their own world or blaming everyone and everything on why they are so depressingly miserable.

But it does not have to be this way for these cheerless, downhearted individuals if they would realize that they too have the potential to lead an abundant and joyful life. The answer lies in living for others and not themselves.

Winning in the game of life

One of my favorite prescriptions for winning the game of life is found in the book *Successful Aging* by John Wallis Rowe M.D. and Robert L. Kahn. They write of the three common characteristics of successful aging which are Move, Manage, and Mingle. This third component, Mingle, is the foundation of Togetherness for DESIGN SMARTS living. The authors explain that being engaged in life and having a purpose is not merely a suggestion, but mandatory to age successfully. But what does this actually mean to be engaged in life and to mingle?

There is no one formula that works for everyone. However, what is predictably considered universally a detriment for unsuccessful aging for the O50s, is living in isolation, self-absorption, and the "my four and no more" life formula. This means being totally absorbed with their own family leaving no emotional or physical time for anyone else outside of their family circle.

Undoubtedly, this last sentence will raise many eyebrows! I can imagine that many of my O50s, reading this book, are thinking what does she mean? How ridiculous is this statement to make my family not my number one priority? And, making families a priority is correct, but to what extent? Does this mean tunnel vision by not seeing the lonely neighbor, the recently divorced, and the struggling single mom or families alone with no extended family?

My four and no more

I remember this incident like it was yesterday when actually it happened over 30 years ago. Bob and I moved away from our extended families to the east coast after college and getting married. Subsequent moves took us to the Bay Area in Northern California where our family thrived enjoying camping, skiing, and in general, loving that California lifestyle. Moving to Kansas was a very challenging transition for me. Bob was immediately immersed in his new career and the kids were finding new friends and activities. A few months after our move, I was savoring picture perfect weather on a beautiful Easter day. Nevertheless, after returning from church, I was really missing my friends and family. Late morning, I saw cars pulling up in front of our home and across the street. I wondered what was happening when wham, I knew in an instant what was happening.

Our neighbor was having an Easter brunch with lots of families and we were not included. We could hear all the kids playing outside while our little family ate our Easter dinner alone. This is what I mean by "my four and no more" if it is exclusively including, or focusing, on a circle of friends and family while being blind to others needs and conditions.

Admittedly, over the past few years, I have not been very aware of others around me being more self-absorbed than I normally prefer to operate. In 2015, Bob's diagnosis of stage 4 melanoma cancer, plus his endless work travel, my own personal and professional travel and work, has left me barely living above water. This is not like me, as my inner circle knows. And this is not what I will continue in our move to Ohio.

Of course, there will be a transition period; but after getting settled in, I have goals and plans to be living the connected life with others again.

But what about Bob?

A slight bunny trail here for an update on Bob's medical status and a little added humor. As he and I were discussing the progress on my writing of this book, he asked me if I mentioned his medical journey these past couple of years. We both started laughing like, duh, "what about Bob?" Well, he did have another scare after being off of his treatment for a year and half with an additional tumor growth. So off Bob went to MDA in Houston while also conferring with our wonderful oncologist in Wichita, Kansas. After resuming his original treatment regimen, the tumors, again, miraculously disappeared. Therefore, the assumption for Bob moving forward is to indefinitely continue his medical routine. What a blessing and a huge sigh of relief to realize we did indeed have a life ahead together. This is what we are standing on, in faith, while planning exactly what giving back will look like for us. In a way, Bob's update is not entirely a bunny trail since his medical status certainly affects what life involvements we could undertake.

How to live a life of joy and fulfillment and TOGETHERNESS

Like myself, I bet you also get lost, at times, in the struggles and strains of life. But in order to get our act together so to speak, it requires all of us to take a good hard look at what we are actually doing routinely with our daily schedules as the years speed by. To avoid living life like we are on autopilot, perhaps consider the following suggestions. Many or all of these TOGETHERNESS activities could make a wonderful new life changing experience for you. As you personally implement your positive changes, compounding this good news for you, undoubtedly, is the exponentially positive effect on many others. You win. They win. Everyone wins and benefits from your new outlook and input as you change your perspective and your actions to:

- Make time for family.
- Make time for friends.
- Schedule time to connect with friends.
- Find meaningful causes or groups to be involved with using your time or your expertise.
- Get out of your personal "to do" lists.
- Loosen up your schedule to experience margin in your days.
- Be proactive in connecting with others by getting out of your comfort zone, out of your routine, and basically just getting out of your home.
- Volunteer your time.
- Find new hobbies like photography or learning to play pickle ball. I plan on doing both!
- Take classes that are free and available to those over 50 or 55 years old.

Sounds like a no brainer, right? Oh, if it were only that easy to change our habits and our routines. Knowledge is the beginning of understanding and wisdom. The O50s with DESIGN SMARTS analyze their actual day to day activities to evaluate how they truly spend their time. Those who choose to live with TOGETHERNESS will leave margin of time for others besides their inner circle. Without a doubt, this is the beginning of wisdom living that will reap exponential joy to be involved in making a difference for others. Knowledge, without wisdom and understanding as we know, will in this context, block anyone to gain and experience the potential for the limitless beautiful possibilities to a rewarding and meaningful life. Sadly, there are just too many people aimlessly traveling through life without a compass. Sadly, for them, but tragic actually, is the loss that their life could have impacted on someone else who was in desperate need for what they possessed.

Therefore, it is simply not enough to be comfortable and secure if we are to live the life that the late President, J.F. Kennedy prescribed. To live a life of authenticity and intentional purpose, we must give back.

You were meant for higher purposes

Regardless of your faith or no faith, hopefully you can agree that no one in the entire universe has your DNA, setting you apart with distinctive gifts, talents, and passions. And likewise, not a single person is equipped with the traits you possess. You can be an influence on all those crossing your life paths. This is such a win-win concept! You win by giving of your specific gifts; and those receiving your gifts will win. I believe that there is a plan and a destiny for every one of us. Truly rich and fulfilling lives only occur when living, reaching, and seeking our specific purpose and destiny. Every single living and breathing person can positively do something to make a difference in their circle of influence, community, church, work place, or neighborhood, regardless of their financial, physical, educational, or geographical status. To truly thrive, we all need an identity and purpose of who we are. And we need to know the gifts and talents within each one of us.

There are remarkably hundreds of examples of even those in prison making a positive contribution by refusing to allow their present circumstance to prevent them from contributing to others and possibly even leaving a legacy. We all have the potential to do, and be, so much more with our lives.

Again, the good news of getting out of our day to day routine and comfort zone and connecting with others regardless of our age or stage, will reap huge benefits in the O50s aging successfully. In Dr. Roger Landry's book, *Live Long, Die Short*, is a masterpiece of wisdom on quality living, and not merely long living. Dr. Landry, like many other experts in the field of aging, firmly believes that it is so important to be involved with others in life at all ages. It is in our very DNA, that we thrive when being with others to the extent that connectedness determines a lower risk of almost all diseases.

For all of the justifications in this TOGETHERNESS chapter, it again verifies that your very own personal formula for successful aging again, depends on you and you alone. I want so badly for you to grasp and implement these principles that I can taste it! In this game called life, you can win, you can take a pass, or you can, unfortunately, take a loss. To all of you DESIGN SMARTS O50s, I know and believe without a single doubt, that you will be a major winner.

Leaving a legacy of Influence

No one told my late mom, Ellen Garrett, that she could not possibly do all that she did way, way back when she was in her forties, fifties, and up into her nineties. She worked outside of the home as a telephone operator during the era of Donna Reed and Ozzie and Harriet, when most moms stayed at home and very few of my friends' moms worked outside the home.

A funny thing occurred in my very late adulthood. It was realizing the fact that we lived on the "other side" of town. Not for a second did this ever register for my economic status, because my mom made life all very normal, exactly like the other moms that never worked outside the home.

Even though she was working full time, it was always my mom who volunteered to be a Brownie and Girl Scout leader, who often made the cookies or brownies, or brought food to tons of school events. I remember fondly that I was a little girl who loved, loved her baby dolls. My dolls had tons and tons of clothes made by, of course, my mom.

A Path to Joyful Living That's Not All About Me

Then I was in junior and senior high and at super fun and memorable slumber parties! You guessed it. They were very often at my house in our basement. And, right again, she always made sloppy Joes, brownies, chip and dip, etc. She let us stay up late, late, late, and never did I hear, "You girls be quiet, I have to work!"

Then I went away to college at Ohio University in Athens, Ohio, four VERY long hours away from my hometown. I still remember thinking how homesick I was, being a small-town girl at a university almost twice the size of my whole town's population.

While Mom was still working full time, my mom and dad and sweet baby sister Kim, would travel to Ohio University as much as their work would allow visiting me. And they were never empty handed on these family visits. Oh no, they were loaded down with, you guessed it, homemade brownies, chocolate chip cookies, fresh lilacs for my birthday month, and new Villager brand knock-off dresses complete with matching headbands sewn, of course, by my mom.

No fast food then, no cleaning ladies, tons of ironing, my little sister still at home—but my mom and dad made it all work. And work they did…very hard. Even as she was pushing ninety years old, she did not slow down to her age acting like someone in her seventies, perhaps.

She would put on her tennis shoes every Monday. And for hours and hours she served the needy at the Community Center in Salem, Ohio. Of course, she was by far the oldest serving those much, much younger than herself. She often confessed to me that she couldn't help herself from sneaking extra cookies to the little ones. Even when she was well into her late eighties you would have found her helping out at the food bank on Fridays, doing, I'm sure, whatever was asked of her.

And for many, many years, she and her friends adopted a group of mentally challenged women, taking them on outings such as bowling, hot dog roasts in the park, movies, doing crafts, or taking them out to eat.

And, if I told you what home baked food, she packed in suitcases to bring to our family, whether she's traveling by car or by plane, you probably would not believe it possible. But believe it. She even kept a notebook of who likes what cookies and quantities and what to adjust for the next family get together...seriously!

Or, would you even believe me, if I told you also that she still exercised and cooked VERY healthy meals for herself, even with my dad being gone for years. She got pretty feisty when she heard people say they won't cook because it is just themselves, or just the two of them. Pity the poor soul that got her started on that one. I loved it!

I haven't even skimmed the surface of all that my mom was, and all that she did, for sooooooooo many people. And my dad, too, was always behind the scenes doing everything that needed to be done when it needed to be done for family and friends alike. Putting up shelves, delivering mom's cooking, washing, washing, washing, and washing tons of pots and pans! Yes, my dad would literally be the one giving "the shirt off his back" type. Tons of family and friends' stories attest to this generous spirit that my dad had too.

As I move into a future of DESIGN SMARTS, Ellen Garrett will always be in the back of my mind saying, "Who said you couldn't do this, Mitzi?" Because no one ever told her, with any success, that she could not accomplish all she did indeed accomplish. May I be half the woman that my mom was. She had shown her entire life that no matter what her circumstances were, she was indeed a woman of influence.

In closing this chapter, it is not about the applause, it is not about the numbers, and it is not about the recognition. No, the O50s who leave a legacy of influence will have an impact on others that will extend way beyond their lifetime. Those O50s giving back will live the happiest and much healthier lives by being busy for others, while taking the focus off of themselves. What a beautiful way to live out the fourth quarter of life.

"Stay connected: it is so important, it's in our very DNA, we thrive being with others. To the extent you are connected, it lowers the risk of almost all diseases."

—*Successful Aging* by Rowe and Kahn

# REFLECTIONS

1. Under the list of how to live a joyful life which 3 of these action items would make a difference for you?

    - Make time for family.
    - Make time for friends.
    - Schedule time to connect with friends.
    - Find meaningful causes or groups to be involved with using your time or your expertise.
    - Get out of your personal "to do" lists.
    - Loosen up your schedule to experience margin in your days.
    - Be proactive in connecting with others by getting out of your comfort zone, out of your routine, and basically just getting out of your home.
    - Volunteer your time.
    - Find new hobbies like photography or learning to play pickle ball. I plan on doing both!
    - Take classes that are free and available to those over 50 or 55 years old.

    _____

    _____

    _____

    _____

2. Besides caring for your family, what are ways you could contribute (not money) in your community, your neighborhood, or other places? _____

_____

_____

_____

S.M.A.R.T.S.

 SPACES. Our spaces directly impact our lives. What is working in your home now? What is not?

 **MINDSETS.** Our lives directly follow our thinking. A positive mindset results in a positive life; a negative mindset results in a negative life. You get to choose.

 **ATTITUDES.** Our attitudes directly affect all and everything we do or become in our life. Age is just a number and you get to choose your attitude toward aging.

 **ROUTINES.** Our personal lifestyle in achieving wellness directly impacts our lives. Are you putting yourself first regarding your own personal life? You get to choose.

 **TOGETHERNESS.** Our relationships directly affect our quality of life. Giving back to your community and others changes everything. You get to choose to live outside of your inner circle connections.

 **SPIRITUAL.** Our personal decisions about spirituality affects our outlook on life. Everyone believes in something—either your own power or a divine power.

SPIRITUALITY

FINISHING PHASE

CHAPTER 17

Everyone Believes in Something

Connecting the Final Dots of DESIGN SMARTS: SPIRITUALITY

Downsizing gives you time to explore and discern what you really be in or whom you believe in. In this final chapter, I will share what very few people know about me.

I remember the day well. It was October 12, 2015 and I walked into the doctor's office to discuss a rather delicate and extremely personal issue. The waiting room bombarded me with mismatched, ugly, green and orange chairs. Wallpaper that made me dizzy and outdared magazines littered everywhere.

Combined with terrible lighting, the outdated awful color palette looked even worse. Interestingly enough, analyzing how bad this waiting room was kept my mind off what I was about to learn. But still, better, more intentional choices might also have made my wait more pleasant.

The Two Types of Power

But first, I cannot complete this manuscript without fully explaining how the last S in the acronym of S.M.A.R.T.S. represents SPIRITUALITY. Without a doubt, it is a POWER that results from choosing to live by the DESIGN SMARTS principles to age better and smarter. This power to live by choice, and not by chance, propels the O50s light years ahead of those who continue to remain the same year after year. In other words, those who choose to live by chance in a mindset of complacency, means reaping a stagnant lifestyle that jeopardizes the health, wellness, and happiness of their future. I accept the fact that millions of O50s may not believe in God or a higher power. Nevertheless, the potential opportunity they have absolutely exists to rock their future years in releasing the Power of living with the DESIGN SMARTS principles to age better and age smarter.

The second meaning of spiritual power, for me personally, is the power that comes from faith. Now I will share with you what very people know about me. For, perhaps, over a ten-year span, I had numerous breast biopsies resulting from, inconclusive but suspicious, mammograms. It's certainly no walk in the park waiting for the lab results of each biopsy. Each time the consult, with the radiologist or my medical doctor, explained to me that there were pre-cancer cells; but none were showing up yet as cancer. It became apparent, with the pattern of these unusual cells, that it was adamantly important to have biopsies every six months. It was like the inevitable feeling of waiting for the other shoe to drop after each test. Therefore, the decision was made to proceed for approval of having a double mastectomy as a preventative procedure.

The reason why I can recall the breast surgeon's waiting room so clearly is that there were two major obstacles to overcome before this surgery could take place. I was seeing this surgeon for the first time having no idea if she would approve the recommended preventive surgery. The second very major obstacle was determining if Medicare would cover the five-figure cost. One could not happen without the other for scheduling this life changing medical procedure.

Why was I so confident that I definitely needed to take this radical step since there was no evidence of actual cancer cells? Additionally, why am I choosing to share this now in this chapter? Without a shadow of a doubt, there was a strong spiritual discernment, or as some would describe it, a still small voice repeatedly advising me that this proactive, preventative surgery indeed had to happen. Both of my obstacles were eventually approved, and a surgery date was set for January of 2016. Understandably, to undertake such an unprecedented and drastic action was viewed a bit rash by some of those who knew. But I never wavered in my resolve that I knew that I knew, this procedure must transpire.

Backing up to that same week of October 12, 2015, I must also share that is when Bob was having a lung biopsy. Also, during this exact same week, I was scheduled to travel on business to High Point Market in North Carolina. Unbeknownst to me when I had agreed months before to be part of the prestigious Interior Designers Bloggers tour, could I have known that it would be the same precise time of these major medical issues.

Being married to a logical, left-brain engineer has it perks when it comes to assessing how to deal with difficult life decisions and challenges. I was very nervous leaving Bob without knowing his test results, but he insisted I fulfill my professional obligation. He wisely convinced me I could accomplish nothing by staying in Wichita. The next day, I traveled to N.C. and again, with total recall, I remember, after just arriving in my hotel room, I got the call that Bob's lung biopsy showed cancer. Thank goodness our daughter lovingly called me first to prepare me before I would talk to Bob. But how do you prepare for lung cancer?

Here I was, all alone in my hotel room in a state of total shock. When I did talk with Bob that evening, the first thing I said was that I was flying home immediately. From the left brainer, was repeated the amazingly sound reasons that to return home would accomplish absolutely nothing, so I stayed. The only way I didn't crumble was to stay in my steel-trap mindset to not utter a word about Bob's situation. There were a few trusted friends at market that I did confide in eventually; but very briefly so as not to make a spectacle of myself by losing it. It just wasn't the time.

Several months later, in January of 2016, I am recovering at home from a double mastectomy not in the least bit concerned about waiting for my lab results. I told my family this was merely routine; and was definitely not a big deal since my surgery was purely a preventative procedure. Here again, I have total recall as the surgeons PA called to give me the lab results. I was in my design studio nonchalantly listening to her when she said the word malignancy. What? There was indeed cancer in a mammary duct that would not likely have been discovered by mammograms or by any of my previous biopsies.

I knew that I had to have the surgery for preventative measures, not if cancer would develop but when it would develop. I had no idea that cancer cells had already started developed. If I had not listened to my inner discerning leading, who knows how far the cancer would have spread before it was detected? Since these cells were in the mammary duct, there wasn't a lump detected or even of any suspicious signs in my last mammogram. Yes, I believe that my family and I were spared from a potentially very difficult road ahead of cancer treatments.

I believe my faith saved me

I must, however, confess that this detailed sharing of my medical information is way out of my comfort zone. However, in this chapter on spirituality, it was listening to that still small voice and believing that I was being led saved me from untold and possible disastrous consequences in my future. What if I hadn't pursued, with an almost determined vengeance, to have this preventative procedure? As it turned out for me, I had to have zero post op treatments of any kind, none whatsoever. My doctors agreed that if these cancer cells were to be unchecked, my outcome would certainly be totally different and not in a positive direction.

Everyone believes in something

I don't discredit those that don't share my faith; so I hope you won't discredit me, and my entire book, in learning that I am a believer, a woman of faith. You see, everyone believes in something. Think about this statement. Where have you placed your hope or belief? Are you putting your believing hope in your investments, your career, your inheritance, your 401K, your company's security, your health or your spouse's income? Yes, whether it is acknowledged or not, everyone believes in something or someone.

I believe in miracles. My dear friend, Adam, says that I am a miracle magnet. I am grateful for all the miracles that have happened for me and are happening in my life, but I am no more special than anyone else. The older I become, perhaps the distinguishing difference between others and me is that I watch, acknowledge, and am thankful for miracles both big and small. I have honed my awareness in miracle watching, in divine protection, healing, nature, and restorations.

Miracles of protection...Out of no where

Another memory, cemented in my brain from early in my marriage, was when my mom and I were shopping inside a Canton, Ohio mall 45 minutes from our hometown of Salem, Ohio. Realize that, then, there were no cell phones. So we shopped all day, having a glorious time together, never, for a second, realizing outside a very significant snowstorm was brewing. After shopping, we started to drive home, the roads were very snow packed and slippery. Trying to not panic, as I attempted to steer an elevated curving entrance ramp to a highway, our car went spinning out of control heading for a cavernous drop off. Out of nowhere, a man opened my driver's door and yelled move over! He recovered the car back to the road, jumped out, and disappeared. As far as my mom and I could see, no car or person was anywhere in sight!

I was in New York City visiting a friend that treated me to a Broadway play. He was wheelchair dependent, so it took us a while, after the play ended, getting to the bus stop several blocks away from the theatre. I remember feeling increasingly unsettled, and actually scared, that we were the only ones, at eleven thirty that evening, waiting at the bus stop. After two bus drivers ignored my waving and sped by us, I was really getting scared. Honest truth, another bus pulled over at the bus stop; but when he noticed my friend in a wheelchair, he started to drive away. Out of nowhere, an angry man came running up to the bus banging and screaming at the bus driver. Finally, the driver opened the door, lowered the lift for my friend, so we were safely on our way to our hotel rooms. As I searched for this man out the window, no one was in sight!

I believe in miracles of healing. To witness Bob living a normal life after a stage-four melanoma cancer diagnosis and to acknowledge that it was a divine discernment to pursue my proactive surgery, supports my faith in healing miracles. I believe in miracles of restoration, like the restoration of our home Cypress that was beyond any hope and our resources. Over and over again, I have witnessed miracles of other's careers, relationships, and finances.

It appeared that my design career was over, like someone turned off a switch to block new design projects from coming my way. Also, while others I knew personally were soaring in their blogging and social media success, my numbers were either stagnating or decreasing. I felt like, Mitzi who? I did, however, reluctantly attend the March 2016 Design Bloggers Conference in my insecure, low self-worth state, to learn what I was doing so wrong. If you recall, my double mastectomy was in January prior to this huge conference, merely a month earlier. I know, what was I thinking? But I had to get out of myself so I could reconnect with our wonderful and supportive community of designers and bloggers. Throughout the days of presentations, I sat by my dear friends, Ruthie and Linda. Realize that I had not yet shared my medical situation to anyone. I just knew it was not the time or place for such a revelation. But Ruthie and Linda felt safe to me as I struggled to maintain some sense of dignity, being at my lowest ever in my career and blogging confidence.

As I fought my feelings of despair and discouragement, with total honesty I can say that I never, ever lost my faith. I didn't play the blame game as I dug into that "now what" question about my design, speaking, and blogging career. You may be asking what any of this has to do with miracles.

It would be another book to recap all that has happened since that conference, but I believe it was another miracle in the lucrative restoration my design career. This book you are holding is an example of what I emphatically believe is a miracle for someone like me being in my 70's.

My faith is not my label

I have and love friends of all backgrounds, skin color, and various diversities. But is agreement a requirement for love? I believe in treating everyone with respect. What I do not believe in is being negative, sarcastic, or angry with those of differing beliefs. Therefore, to use social media as a platform for mean spirited comments, to me, is inappropriate, regardless which side of the isle in D.C. to which someone is connected. One of the saddest changes I see in America today is our loss of tolerance for those that believe or think differently than we do. If you knew how many friends, I have that are atheists, gay, liberal, ultra-conservative, or agnostic, you would be very surprised. And these friends of mine, in turn, respect what I believe, which, in many areas, is totally opposite of what they believe, or do not believe.

Millions were hurt by their religious upbringing

As we have been expounding on how much America has and is changing since the O50s have been born, without a doubt, our culture has seen the biggest changes. It is hard for my grandchildren to even believe we had to actually get out of our chair to change the TV channel! And speaking of TV, I vividly remember Ozzie and Harriet and other major TV stars in twin beds on the rare shots that we even saw them in their bedrooms. Furthermore, it was considered the unusual family that didn't attend church or at least take their kids and drop them off at Sunday school. Some of my most fun times in junior high were going to whatever church youth group was having a dance or hay ride or roller-skating party. I was there, and so were all my friends, no matter what church they went to, if even they didn't go to church at all.

The Spirituality of DESIGN SMARTS is not of laws or religion.

However, now in America, the Pew Research polls tell us that it is the minority of Americans who are attending church. Our culture has all but said "we do not need religion anymore." I do not think we need religion either if it is a dogma of rules and guilt producing, condemning religious practices. And this is exactly why I personally believe so many O50s left the church and will never darken another church door again. It sounds so superficially fake, but I sincerely hope and pray the O50s can reconsider their faith philosophies if they can know us by our love, even with those with whom we disagree.

And yet millions of Americans are again seeking faith by returning to their churches, small groups or their own spiritual paths as the world gets crazier and crazier. The difference to me, in a sustaining faith, is again quite simple. It gives my life purpose. My personal belief is that if we truly are believers, our lives show it in intentional living and giving to others. It is not about the "bless my four and no more."

My mustard seed of faith

I received a bracelet in junior high that has a mustard seed charm with a verse engraved on the back. Miraculously, I still have that bracelet today, over fifty years later. This bracelet becomes exponentially more significant to me as I had a lifetime of mountain moving experiences. You see my faith is not merely my label, my faith directs my life. There is a saying, "go to the throne, not the phone". Translated, so to speak, this means not running to the phone to rehearse all the awful things someone said, or the latest drama that is unfolding. By being repeated over and over, issues and problems not only steal our joy but they affect our health. How could this be? Every single thought we have, whether positive or negative, releases 100 chemicals in our body. Spinning minds also block our creativity and productivity. Going to the throne means entering into the rest of God and not trusting ourselves to take care or control of each and every issue coming at us.

An example of entering into this rest occurred after hearing of Bob's extremely serious diagnosis. Many close to me though that I was either in denial, or was being extremely selfish, by not showing any meltdowns. What would have been accomplished by my having a melt down? Would it have been better accepted to hear me saying, "Oh my gosh, he's not going to make it!" Or, "What is going to happen to my life and future?"

Admittedly worry, doubt and anxiety were my best friends for way, way too long. But now, I refuse to live my life in those distressed mindsets any longer. It is no secret to those in my inner circle that I start every single day in what I call my quiet time. With my carefully selected devotionals, this early morning time equips, enlightens, and empowers me for my day ahead. I must renew my mind every single day. I accept that this is adamantly more critical today for me with all that is happening in my life along with these turbulent and uncertain times in the world of today.

Wrapping up connecting the dots

As I was determining how and what areas to include when writing this book, and what to address for obtaining a DESIGN SMARTS life, going back to the basics was the only authentic answer for what to share. I believe that all three—mind, body, and spirit—are part of who we all are.

So, as we are looking at all the areas of the acronym **SMARTS**—**S**paces, **M**indsets, **A**ttitudes, **R**outines, **T**ogetherness, and **S**pirituality—not to reinforce how all the areas of mind, body, and spirit are included could be incomplete and inconclusive without reinforcing the repetition that all of these categories are totally essential in my beliefs on how to live the vibrant, ageless life.

Those with Designer Smarts will seek to:

- Get out of debt
- Get healthy
- Get organized
- Get prepared

Rewards of those living with Design Smarts:

- Will enjoy a simpler lifestyle
- Will be grateful
- Will be generous
- Will love unconditionally

In closing, the main thing is the main thing which is to understand how essential it is to implement these DESIGN SMARTS principles in daily life. The entire message of this book can be summed up in two words: GET Ready!

I believe that now in your very own personal preparations for what is ahead for you, that you know how the Design SMARTS in:

- Your updated SPACES can elevate your life to a higher level
- Your updated MINDSETS can open up new doors of exciting possibilities
- Your updated ATTITUDE can make an astounding difference in your life
- Your updated ROUTINE can give you greater longevity and quality of life
- Your upgraded TOGETHERNESS can be a win- win for you and many others
- Your upgraded SPIRITUALITY can help you discern what or whom you believe in

My final questions for you O50s to ponder is to ask yourself

Is your home **SPACE** nurturing?

Is your **MINDSET** empowering?

Is your **ATTITUDE** enlightening?

Is your **ROUTINE** equipping?

Is your **TOGETHERNESS** connecting?

Is your **SPIRIT** discerning?

The stakes are simply too high choosing by default to a live life of chance with a complacent, naïve attitude and mindset. To me there is nothing more gratifying than observing those light bulb moments through possibility thinking. See your life with a fresh vision to live a rewarding life by your goal oriented intentional choices. Your life of calculated choices will have a rippling effect to everything and everyone in your family or friendship circle of influence, exactly like a skipping stone across the water. Yes, your next years could indeed be your very best years.

 **REFLECTIONS**

1. This chapter discusses two types of power. The first type of power is from living life with DESIGN SMARTS. What are your top 3 areas that inspired or motivated you to personally make life changes in each of these important areas?

    Spaces   Mindsets   Attitudes

    Routines   Togetherness   Spirituality

2. The second type of power refers to a spiritual power. Again, for your eyes only, what thoughts were meaningful for you?

Conclusion

I believe, with all my heart, that your tenacity, effort, discipline, and sacrifice will reap great rewards for you to live the sought after exciting, vibrant life full of delightful adventures and unexpected, fabulous experiences. I hope that you will have no regrets and go for it all. After all, what do you have to lose?